MORE
GLIMPSES
of HEAVEN

Books by Trudy Harris

Glimpses of Heaven

MORE GLIMPSES
of HEAVEN

Inspiring True Stories of Hope and
Peace at the End of Life's Journey

Trudy Harris, RN

Revell

a division of Baker Publishing Group
Grand Rapids, Michigan

Published by Revell
a division of Baker Publishing Group
P.O. Box 6287, Grand Rapids, MI 49516-6287
www.revellbooks.com

Printed in the United States of America

Library of Congress Cataloging-in-Publication Data
Harris, Trudy.
    More glimpses of heaven : inspiring true stories of hope and peace at the end of life's journey / Trudy Harris.
        p.   cm.
    ISBN 978-0-8007-3440-4 (pbk.)
    1. Death—religious aspects—Christianity. I. Title.
BT825.H2855 2010
236'.1—dc22   2010025699

In keeping with biblical principles of creation stewardship, Baker Publishing Group advocates the responsible use of our natural resources. As a member of the Green Press Initiative, our company uses recycled paper when possible. The text paper of this book is comprised of 30% post-consumer waste.

green press INITIATIVE

10   11   12   13   14   15   16   7   6   5   4   3   2   1

For all those whom God sent to our care. They taught us life's lessons along the way.

Through God's grace alone, we prepared one another for the ultimate promise of eternal life by sharing the experience of His presence in our everyday lives.

In loving memory of Robert Gura, Jimmy Gillespie, Marie Pendley, George Fipp, Buddy Neviaser, Maureen Offord, and Father John O'Hara. Their meaningful and wonderful lives touched ours in very profound ways. We will always miss them.

Conversations . . .

Look at Me and no one else,
See none but Me, My child.
Compare not yourself to others now,
Consider Me awhile.

Do not be distracted by anyone, anything,
Look past all else to Me.
I will show you all I have
And all I want you to be.

Spend time with Me, My little one,
The rush should stop for now.
Listen to Me softly speak to you,
I will show you how.

So many things get in the way,
Time speeds by, you see.
Soon it will be over for you, My child,
What will be will be.

So much work yet to be done,
I need your hands, your heart.
Listen carefully while I tell you so,
My wisdom and gentleness I impart.

Trudy Harris

Contents

Contents

Contents

Contributors' Stories

Bonnie Tingley, RN, Hospice nurse
Dorothy • Sarah • Jim • Todd • Matthew • Marsha • Cathy

Ede Pearson Huston, RN, Hospice nurse
David • Tom

Nancy M. Powers, personal friend
Ed

Annie Rini, ARNP, pediatric nurse
Joni

Cookie Schnier, RN, Hospice nurse
Mr. Winters

Dottie Dorion, RN, BSN, Hospice founder
Lois

Jackie Aquino, RN, Hospice nurse
Luke • Jessica

Helen K. Basile, RN
Joseph

Bonnie Morris, RN, pediatric Hospice nurse
Donny

Dianne Rigby, RN, BSN, Hospice nurse
James

Nikki Fox-Nash, Hospice volunteer department
Douglas

Lois-Anne Isabelle, RN, Hospice professional education coordinator
Ronald

Gene H. Lewis, RN, Hospice founder
Charlie

Judith Lothman, RN, BSN, Hospice nurse
Sam

Susie Russell, Hospice volunteer program specialist
Levi

Acknowledgments

I gratefully acknowledge my husband, George, who is God's greatest lifetime gift to me. It is only through his unfailing faithfulness, patience, and love that this book has been written.

To our sons, George and Kenneth, and their families, whose good humor and confidence helped me on a daily basis. Special thanks to sons Jon and Erik, whose computer and word skills and patience enabled me to complete both *Glimpses of Heaven* and *More Glimpses of Heaven*. It would not have been possible without them.

In loving memory of my parents, Peggy and John Horan, whose lifetime of faith-filled living laid the foundation for the future of each of their children. A special thanks to my sisters Peggy and Anne. Sharing their most intimate and loving memories made the writing of my sister Maureen's story possible.

To Sister Naureen Marie, who, as my earliest guide in the field of compassionate nursing care, taught me to see Christ in every patient I was called to serve. Her constant reminder of "Jesus loves you, little one" spurred me on through years of living in and out of the nursing profession.

I gratefully acknowledge all those who enthusiastically contributed stories of the dying patients in their care. These dedicated nurses and Hospice workers teach us about Jesus's compassion and love and reflect His presence in our everyday lives. Each one is an outstanding person in their own right, and the profession of nursing is blessed to have them in its midst.

Many people today are open to the discussion of death and dying because of the earliest pioneers in Hospice care and those in small Hospice programs throughout the United States. They took down, in one way or another, the mystery surrounding the most natural phenomenon of life and covered it with the grace and simplicity that God intended. They sought to present the dying patient as a physical, emotional, and spiritual being and helped us understand that addressing the patient as a "whole person" is vital to a peaceful transition when life is ending. We owe them a debt of gratitude for the goodness, tenacity, and consistency of their message. They changed the way we approach the inevitable, our own dying time and that of our loved ones and friends. They are too numerous to name here, but they know well who they are and can rest in the knowledge that their untiring efforts brought enlightenment and understanding to the process of dying. They showed us the way to peace.

Carol Susan Roth, my agent, worked tirelessly on my behalf and enthusiastically represented me in all the best ways possible, providing encouragement every step of the way. Carol died on February 8 surrounded by her loving family and friends. She told me a few days before she died that she felt destined to represent me with both *Glimpses of Heaven* and *More Glimpses of Heaven*, coming to a new and deeper understanding of God in the process. Carol was a loving and trusted friend, and I will always miss her and be grateful to her.

Introduction

We see and experience God more often than we know. He often hides in plain sight, and we encounter Him many more times a day than we realize, in the people and experiences He puts on our path. When Jesus said, "The kingdom of God is at hand," was He asking us to recognize His presence and that of His Father in our everyday living? Do we allow ourselves the silence He calls us to in order to sit still long enough to see and hear Him?

The term "kingdom of God" has always been one of my favorite biblical phrases. In my mind, it means that wherever and whenever God's presence is seen, recognized, or experienced by His people, God is there in the midst of them. When we see love in action, compassion in the face of hatred or anger, forgiveness in the face of pain and suffering, we are looking at and experiencing the kingdom of God right where we stand. How wonderful that our Jesus, fully human, fully divine, invites us to participate with Him in the kingdom of God here and now, every day.

I heard a young priest's homily recently, during which he asked us where Jesus could be found in our lives. He spoke about recognizing Him in the marketplace, among the people, in the face of the man who stands by the highway every morning begging, and in those we judge to be "less" than what we think they should be. He encouraged us to look carefully in the Scriptures and see how often God's reign or kingdom was with the poor, the outcasts, and those who lived on the fringes of society. The priest said that in order to find the Jesus we are looking for and to love and follow Him, we must be looking in all the same places Jesus spent His time. If we do not find Him, we must ask ourselves why. When Jesus died, He left us a very clear blueprint to follow. He told us, in the simplest terms possible, that the greatest among us must serve the least, and that in serving others we would really be serving Him.

My earliest recollections are of my parents doing things for others. My mother bringing into our family the child of her dearest friend, when this friend died very young. My dad carrying a co-worker to the car each morning when he could no longer walk. By example, my parents taught us so well to serve others that, for me, Hospice nursing was simply an extension of the life they had lived. Hospice nursing is the purest kind of nursing you can do, and every day you are reminded that you walk on holy ground in preparing God's children for heaven. Hospice nursing is very intimately participating in the kingdom of God that Jesus spoke about.

In *Glimpses of Heaven: True Stories of Hope and Peace at the End of Life's Journey*, I shared the stories of God's intimate involvement with His children and reflected on how often He allows them to hear His voice deep within their souls as they are dying. As often as these experiences occur, at the end of life, God invites us on a daily basis to look for and recognize how He manifests Himself through the needs of others. He shows us how we who are well are called to be His eyes and His ears, His hands and His heart, to those who are not, every day. In order to become one with Jesus and to "put on Christ" as Paul directs us to, we must walk in the footsteps He puts right in front of us to follow.

The publication of *Glimpses of Heaven* brought an avalanche of letters from other professionals in the field of

Hospice and palliative care nursing, expressing their own tender and moving accounts of caring for people as they were dying. They were thrilled to see in writing the same kind of experiences they shared with those at the end of life in their care. They too felt equally blessed to have the opportunity to prepare patients to meet their God and to find the peace He was longing to give them.

More Glimpses of Heaven includes more of my own experiences and stories shared with me by other professionals in the field of Hospice and end-of-life care. Each one is a real-life account of a patient who was dying, and in each instance, the caregiver sensed something greater than themselves at work. These stories lend credence to the belief that when our time arrives, we will not be alone. I remember well hearing these stories told by many of the nurses when we gathered for Hospice team meetings in the past. I am most grateful to them for recounting their experiences here for you.

In these stories you will find God's loving presence reflected in both the lives of those He is calling home to Himself as well as those caring for them. Look for the compassion, forgiveness, generosity, and tenderness of Jesus's own heart. Do you recognize Him in those who make life easier and more peaceful for others as they are both living and dying? Do you see His humanity and humor reflected through their kindness? He shows us His face in our everyday lives, and if we pay attention, we will see and hear Him. He is inviting us to become part of the kingdom of God here on earth—and what a wonderful invitation it is!

Author's note: the names, diagnoses, and histories of those portrayed here have been changed to protect their privacy. In those instances where families have asked that the real names of their loved ones be used, I have done so.

Sally

"He wanted her to see herself as beautiful one last time"

Trudy Harris

She was so young and lovely, in her late twenties, but she was dying of cervical cancer, which had spread to many parts of her body. There were no more treatments left that would give her more time or make her well again. Her cancer was fast growing, and nothing, not all the love in the world, could change the fact that Sally was going to die.

Her husband, who loved her more than life itself, was heartbroken as he dealt with the reality of life without her in it. He could not comprehend that his two small children would never remember the woman he loved so much and the one who had loved them all well.

He had so much to handle—a job to keep everything going, small children to tend to, a wife to love until there were no more days left for them, and plans to make without her help.

Sally's pain was such that it could no longer be controlled at home, and so the decision was made to take her to the Hospice Center, where she could be more comfortable and pain free. As hard as the decision was to make, it was the right one and everyone knew it, most of all Sally. At the Hospice Center, family could come and go, taking turns staying with her. Children could visit for short periods of time throughout the day, and things would be more peaceful and serene for them. Her husband could work during the day, which he very badly needed to do, and stay most nights with her while his parents took care of their children.

Time was fleeting, and it became more evident every day that Sally's young life was ebbing away quickly. She had always been lovely, and to her husband, she still was, but he wanted her to see herself as beautiful one last time. He wanted her to know that she was still beautiful in his eyes and that she always would be. He needed and wanted time alone with her, just the two of them. He asked if he could bathe her alone, and shampoo and blow-dry her hair. He wanted to cover her frail body with her favorite lotion and dress her in her lovely nightgown and robe one last time.

A special bathing room for just such an occasion had been donated to the Hospice Center when it first opened; everything was carefully prepared for this special time, for Sally and her husband.

Special lamps were brought in and dimmed, soft music was playing some of her favorite songs on the CD player, warm water with delicious bath salts was running in the whirlpool bath, and her favorite blue and white gown and robe were hung by the door for her to see.

Her husband brought Sally to the special bathing room in a wheelchair. He lovingly placed her in the delicious-smelling bath with warm, flowing water. He closed the door behind them; it stayed that way for more than an hour.

When it opened again, Sally was smiling from ear to ear, with freshly shampooed and brushed hair. The wonderful body lotion made her skin glisten from top to bottom, and her gown and robe lay softly on her tiny frame. Together she and her husband looked like two young people forever in love. Time stood still for all of us who were watching.

He loved her with a Christlike love, unselfishly and totally devoid of any concern for himself. He wanted her to know that he would always love her and treasure the memory of the love she had for him, in spite of the few short years they'd had to share. He wanted her to see herself as he saw her, as beautiful as ever. And she was.

The medical and nursing staff stepped back that day and took a deep breath, recognizing the depth of love this young husband had for his dying wife—loving, tender, and completely centered on her.

One cannot help but see Jesus in these most exquisite moments, moments given to us to help us understand how to love as He loves. Sally died a short time later, understanding completely that God is love and where love is, that's where God abides.

Marie

"Oh, darlin', either way I win"

Trudy Harris

Marie was a tiny, five-foot-two, green-eyed southern gal
with curly brown hair and a vivacious spirit and sense of
humor like no one I had ever met. We lived across the driveway from one another when my husband and I moved from
New York to North Carolina. We had much in common,
as we were both young nurses newly working in the field
of hospital medicine. We instantly became lifelong friends,
though two more different people never existed.

Marie was a Charlotte native who was up front and clear,
and spoke her mind. A Southern Baptist, she attended
church faithfully on Wednesday nights and Sunday morn-
ings. As outgoing and friendly as Marie was, her husband,
Fred, was a quiet, slow-talking gentleman from Calhoun,
Georgia, with a sense of humor equal to hers.

Marie had never personally known any "Yankees" before, and the fact that my husband and I were Catholics
was even more intriguing to her. Knowing that we went to

confession, prayed the Rosary, and so on, boggled her mind, but she was always interested in our faith, and we shared many good conversations over the years of our friendship. One of our Catholic practices that gave Marie an impish joy was meatless Fridays. Back in the early 1960s, Fridays were still days on which we did not eat meat (a sacrifice to remind us of the death of Jesus Christ on Good Friday). Marie reveled in lighting up the charcoal grill to cook her thick, juicy hamburgers or hotdogs and calling across the driveway to my husband to let us know we could use the grill for our fish as soon as they were finished. The humor of it all was never lost on anyone.

We were young and quite poor in those days. Marie and Fred owned the grill and washing machine; my husband and I owned the vacuum cleaner and television. We shared everything, and parents from either side could find us in each other's homes, using the shared equipment any time of the day or night. My mother, visiting from New York one afternoon, let herself into our apartment only to find Fred watching television and getting ready to leave with the vacuum. Such was our wonderful friendship.

One Sunday when Marie and Fred were attending church (their Baptist services lasted three to four hours), I forgot to put the hose in the sink while I was doing laundry in their washing machine. When Marie came home, her entire living room was floating on a bed of soapsuds, and it took all four of us the rest of the day to clean it up. Marie told me years later that she had to "lean upon the Lord" and every lesson He had ever taught her to get through that mess and to forgive me. But forgive me she did.

Marie and I had our babies at about the same time, were in the delivery rooms for one another, stayed close, and shared many a prayer during both good times and bad. Although we did not see each other often during our different moves in and out of the area, we remained once-in-a-lifetime friends.

Marie worked her entire adult life in a hospital setting as floor nurse, supervisor, and educator, and she wore any hat needed to further the cause of good nursing care in a large medical center in Charlotte, North Carolina.

In every aspect of her life she applied the love of Jesus Christ. She shared Him with abandon, and over the years we had many, many rollicking conversations about the things we understood differently and the things we understood in the same way, growing each other in faith, never with any animosity at all.

Marie had fought through several bouts of cancer, always moving through her experiences with a confidence borne of deep faith and trust in Jesus Christ. One experience stands out above all the rest. Beside her breast cancer and her kidney cancer (both ultimately removed), Marie had a tumor in the aorta of her heart. Her physician explained that she had a fifty-fifty chance of making it through the surgery, but Marie neither felt nor expressed one iota of concern. Her surgeon explained to a room filled with Marie's church friends that the surgery would take four to five hours, and that she could easily die on the operating table. This was a faithful and prayerful group, and they depended on more than the surgeon's words. They had God on their side.

Before surgery, Marie gave her surgeon a picture, which he kept in his scrubs during surgery. The picture was of Jesus in an operating room, with his hands beneath the surgeon's, reflecting Marie's and everyone's prayer that Jesus Himself would perform her surgery. When the surgeon came into the waiting room less than an hour later, everyone's hearts stopped, fearing the worst. But God had a different plan. The surgeon explained that before he made the cut into the aorta, he had put into place a few safety measures just in case things did not go well. He also had a cardiac surgeon at the ready. He then carefully made the most difficult and risky incision into Marie's aorta, and the tumor simply slipped into his fingers, with no effort at all on his part. He was as much in awe about what had happened as those who were now listening to him. Marie sent me a copy of the picture of Jesus in the operating room, which I treasure to this day.

By early 2008 Marie's cancer of the breast, cancer of the kidney, and other medical challenges had taken their toll on her. She was on full peritoneal dialysis by this time, as she had no kidney function left. She was in and out of the hospital, always attracting people around her with the same humor and faith she had exhibited her entire life, but now she was declining. She spoke of her pastor and how faithful and kind he had always been to her. Her friends cherished her dearly, and not a day went by that they were not visiting and loving her in the full measure with which she had loved them.

In spite of everything, she had made up her mind to come to Jacksonville, Florida, to surprise me at my first public book signing for *Glimpses of Heaven*. I do not think I ever saw a bigger smile or happier person in my life than when I saw her as she walked in the door. I was thrilled to see her and Fred and could barely believe they had driven seven hours to get there with her dialysis equipment in tow. She regaled everyone near her with stories of our younger days together and was loved immediately by everyone who was listening.

Fred had been a loving and faithful husband to Marie for more than forty-nine years, and they cherished each other in the tenderest ways possible. They were true friends and shared a sense of humor about almost everything and could be found laughing together even under the direst of circumstances. She adored her daughters, Kimberly and Allison, and their families, and she received back all the affection and love she had showered on them all their lives.

One afternoon when we were speaking on the phone, she asked when I could get up to see her, and I promised in the next two weeks, as my daughter-in-law was having surgery in her city at that time. I did not realize just how close Marie was to going to heaven. In the most gentle and intimate tone, she told me how much she had always loved me. The conversation felt like Mary's visit with her cousin Elizabeth as told in Scripture, when they were totally dependent on and trusting in the God who loved them. She spoke in the very same way now, trusting that she was safe in His care no matter what, and longing to see Him face-to-face if that was His will. "Oh, darlin'," she said to me in her sweetest southern drawl, "either way I win. If I get through this episode and go home, then I win because I will have more time with Fred and the girls. If I don't get through this episode, then I win anyway, because I will be with my Lord and Savior, and I know that will be everything He promised me it would be."

She spoke of lifelong friendships and how God ordains them for His very own purposes. It was one of the most loving conversations I have ever had with a friend, and I remember it, word for word, to this day. Marie died a few days later surrounded by her family and friends, and safe in the arms of her Lord and Savior Jesus Christ. She had proclaimed Him to everyone she ever met all her life, and now she would see Him face-to-face for all eternity. I am more than certain that when He saw her coming, He went out to meet her, knowing that whatever she had to say would bring a smile to His face.

Donny

"It will be okay, Miss Bonnie, you don't have to cry"

Bonnie Morris

In the order of things in this world, we know that our children are supposed to outlive us. When some of us find out personally that this is not the case, the pain of that knowledge is truly unbearable. All the hopes and dreams we have for our children are severely challenged the moment a diagnosis of a life-threatening illness is made. The question of "why" evolves into hope that treatment somehow will be successful. Days, weeks, and months of pain and struggle are intermingled with prayers, as sometimes things get better and sometimes they do not. The journey can take years, but sometimes it is only months, weeks, or days. In some cases, the day arrives when the doctor can do no more and recommends a Hospice program to support and comfort the child and his family.

It is more than difficult for families to realize that their precious child's journey is ending. A children's Hospice program is specifically structured to help meet the many and varied needs of the entire family. Moms, dads, sisters, brothers, grandparents, aunts, uncles, and cousins all need help and encouragement. Of course, there are the actual physical needs of the child, and pain control is often a large part of that concern. The family may need help with tasks such as getting groceries or helping Dad find a different job that will give him greater flexibility in caring for the family. Brothers or sisters may feel left out because so much attention is directed toward the sick child. The pediatric Hospice team, which includes a pediatric physician, nurse, social worker, chaplain, and volunteer, becomes an integral part of the family's greater structure. Together they act as a support system surrounding the entire family. This support system is a very real expression of God's hand, as He moves to help the family through a time He knows is not going to be easy.

No matter what your religious faith, dying is a spiritual journey. To me there is no one in whom this experience can be seen more clearly than in a child. From the youngest child to the oldest teenager, each has their own way of making this journey. The very young exhibit a total confidence and lack of fear. The older ones seem to have more concerns, but most of these concerns involve their parents and how they will get along without them. Children usually do not talk directly about dying, but if you listen closely, you will hear many clues that tell you they are aware of their journey in a unique way. They tend to look at their world on a day-by-day basis, often sharing even their future dreams with you. This sharing allows you to enter their inner world of both today and tomorrow and walk this intimate and final journey with them. There is no magical formula for this process; it simply requires prayer for the Holy Spirit's direction and quiet listening to His voice.

Each child and family in my care has deeply affected my life in unique ways, and I will be forever grateful to them for allowing me to share in this difficult but precious time in their lives. When I think of all of them, the memories are mingled with laughter and tears, sadness and great joy. It was difficult to let each child go when the time came for them to die. I prayed frequently and with passion for God to keep them with their families, and when the end of their lives was near, I prayed for all of us to let them go and send them off with the knowledge that God would look out for everyone they loved.

One of the youngest in my care was a little three-year-old named Donny. He had been diagnosed with leukemia, and the Children's Tumor Clinic, at the hospital, referred Donny and his family to us when all his treatment options had been exhausted. All of the referrals coming to us from the Tumor Clinic were made with a heavy heart. Calling in Hospice meant that these precious lives were now coming to the last stage of their journey. It was difficult for everyone to accept this reality, and physicians often suffer the most. Over the period of treatment, pediatric oncologists become close to the children and families they serve. Often, when the child dies, they feel they have somehow failed, which is not the case—but a very human response nonetheless. They trust Hospice to share and support in this last period of time for the child and family, and it is indeed a most precious trust they bestow on us.

My journey with my new young friend and his family began in a way I will never forget. I had probably spent only ten or fifteen minutes with Donny when he explained to me casually that Jesus came to visit him sometimes. I asked him what he and Jesus did when He visited. Donny looked at me with smiling eyes and announced that they played together and that Jesus told him everything would be fine.

I was not Donny's regular nurse, so I did not get to see him on a weekly basis. I did get to see him when he and his mother and older brother visited the Tumor Clinic at the hospital. The staff there knew what a joy this young child was to everyone, so they frequently called me to say he would be coming for a checkup. Sometimes, too, Donny and his family would cross the street to my Hospice office, and we would spend time together. I had many stuffed animals around my desk, and sometimes we would all wind up sitting on the floor playing with them. A very large bear sat in the corner of my crowded office, and I always found it interesting that it was the parents who would go to that bear and find themselves curled up in its lap. We never get too old to need love and assurance.

The Tumor Clinic continued to treat Donny while Hospice supported him through all the inevitable changes that were happening to him. Then a phone call one morning announced that treatment was just not working and would be stopped. Time was running out for my bright-eyed friend. With a heavy heart, I walked across the street to the Tumor Clinic. Everyone had their professional behavior in place. The family needed help at this moment, but it was painful for everyone who had loved and cared for them.

My young friend and I went out into the large hallway of the hospital, and he motioned for me to crawl under one of the benches with him. He was excited and wanted me to know that Jesus came to visit him "all the time now." We talked a little about this, and he made it clear that Jesus wanted him to know that his mom, dad, and brother would all be okay. In his special three-year-old vocabulary, he said that Jesus wanted him to know that on one of His visits, He would take Donny with Him into heaven, and Donny was very excited about that. I let him know that when Jesus came for him, he should take Jesus's hand and go with Him. I tried to tell him in terms a three-year-old could understand that all of us would take special care to look after his family. We all would miss him very much, but we would see him again someday. At this point tears were rolling down my face. My young friend reached over, wiped my tears, and assured me, "It will be okay, Miss Bonnie, you don't have to cry." That was the last time I saw Donny. He blessed my life in a way that has no words. I will never forget the joy and total trusting faith he exhibited to all of us.

When people ask me about faith and the reality of Jesus Christ, I have only to think of Donny and share his simple but eloquent message with them.

Evelyn

"God is making your place in heaven, and you will be with Him today"

Trudy Harris

As part of my church ministry, I take Holy Communion to those who are sick and unable to get to church on Sunday. I visit them in their own homes, nursing homes, Hospice centers, or wherever they are living. Catholics find great meaning and comfort in Jesus's words, "Take and eat, this is My body; take and drink, this is My blood."

One Sunday morning, I was visiting an assisted-living facility to bring Holy Communion to Evelyn, who had made her home there for many years. She had no living relatives and had been alone in the world for more years than she wanted to remember. She never complained and was a sweet soul, but you could tell that the feeling of being alone never left her. She longed to belong and to feel loved again.

When I entered the room, Evelyn smiled at me, knowing why I was there. She seemed quite pale and a good bit frailer than the week before. She was resting on her side and speaking barely above a whisper.

Often there appears in a dying person's eyes a look that I call "knowing." The person reflecting that look is often trying hard to see if you "see" what is happening to them. Their eyes are searching your eyes, and when they "see" that you understand and are with them, the relief they reflect is unmistakable.

Evelyn had that look in her eyes that morning, and so the words of the prayers said during this special time took on new meaning. The prayers are always from the New Testament, with Matthew, Mark, Luke, and John telling us about Jesus offering us salvation and inviting us to follow Him. These prayers express enormous compassion, forgiveness, and love and provide great comfort to anyone hearing them, especially a person who is dying.

That particular day, the New Testament words became for Evelyn more alive and meaningful than they ever had before. They held new understanding and promise, and she took each one in as I read them slowly to her. It seemed that Jesus had spoken them just for her today.

The readings spoke to Evelyn of God's plans for those who love and follow Him. Evelyn had tried to do that all her life and had taken to heart His teachings when He said, "I will not leave you orphans; I will come to you" (John 14:18). She understood and believed, too, that when we are sorry for doing wrong and repent, Jesus forgives us entirely. "As far as the east is from the west, so far has he put our transgressions from us" says the Lord (Ps. 103:12). She learned early to always take Him at His word, and it gave great peace to her soul now.

After the prayers were said and she'd had a quiet time with her Lord, I felt prompted to tell her that the very words Jesus had spoken two thousand years ago were about to come true for her. I reminded her that He said, "If I go and prepare a place for you, I will come back again and take you to myself, so that where I am you also may be" (John 14:3). I told her I felt He had chosen these special New Testament readings for her to hear today so she could be comforted and prepared to meet Him. "God is making your place in heaven," I said to her, "and you will be with Him today." Her eyes lit up, and a sweet "knowing" smile crossed her lips as she nodded in agreement. I told her I would pray for her all day long until I heard she was safely in heaven with Him. As I left the room, Evelyn squeezed my hand gently.

It never ceases to amaze me how the Holy Spirit speaks through us clearly in instances like this one. On my own, I would not have had the insight or the courage to tell Evelyn that she would die that very day. When the Holy Spirit works through you, you know it. You step out boldly, knowing it is not you but Him working through you to comfort His children.

I stopped at the nurses' station just outside her door to tell the nurse that Evelyn was dying. "Oh, we're all dying, honey," she said, "we just never know when." The nurse was none too happy when I insisted that Evelyn was in the process of dying now. I asked if someone could go in and be with her. She promised she would go herself, and headed toward Evelyn's room as I turned to leave.

When I arrived home twenty minutes later, the phone rang. It was the nurse who had gone into Evelyn's room. "She died," she said. "She looked so peaceful, just like an angel. How did you know?" I told her about the Holy Spirit and about praying for and listening to His promptings. It is a gift He makes available to us, just as Jesus promised, and no one should go through life without it. Simply say, "Come, Holy Spirit, be with me," and the words will be given to you.

Sam

"See that little girl sitting in the chair? She is here to help me die"

Judith Lothman

I first saw Sam, an elderly Jewish man, as he was being wheeled into a room at the Hospice Center for Caring. Although he was weak, pale, and short of breath, he tried hard to smile when I introduced myself as his nurse. Sam had been a Hospice patient for just about two months, and one of our Hospice nurses was caring for him in his own home, where he wanted to stay. He also had two personal caregivers, Susan and Connie, with him 24/7, one of whom accompanied him on admission into the Hospice Center. His Hospice nurse arrived shortly after with a full report on how he had been doing in the home setting. If you are looking for God's face in everyday life, you have only to look at the Hospice nurses who cared for Sam and the caregivers who never left his side.

At ninety years of age, Sam was in the end stages of congestive heart failure, with all its accompanying discomforts and anxieties. More often than not, patients with congestive heart failure are very weak, tired, and shaky, and therefore unable to take a deep breath. They fear not getting enough oxygen into their lungs. Caring for them requires a great deal of know-how—and patience and compassion as well. Their inability to breathe deeply causes increased anxiety, which in turn causes them not to be able to breathe as easily.

Although Sam had around-the-clock, hands-on caregivers, as well as the Hospice nurses coming to his house, his eighty-six-year-old wife, Martha, had grown increasingly fearful of the idea of Sam dying in their home. By now, she was very weary herself (and many older people have strong feelings about being alone with a loved one when they are dying). We understood Martha's fears and tried to reassure her as best we could. Sam very much wanted to remain at home to die and was sad at the possibility of doing otherwise. But as his dying time drew closer, Martha became even more fearful and anxious.

After much discussion with the medical director, primary nurse, and social worker, we decided to move Sam to the Hospice Center just a few minutes away. His wife and caregivers were in full agreement. The Hospice team caring for him at home and the Hospice Center staff worked together to make the transfer as comfortable and seamless as possible for both Sam and Martha.

Serving the needs of terminally ill and dying patients in a Hospice facility is different from caring for them in their own homes. The Hospice nurse is a guest in the home of the dying patient—a caring visitor, so to speak. In that setting, the patient is able to maintain some control over what is going on around them and what is happening to them. At this stage in the patient's life, so many responsibilities of personal care have been taken over by others, and often the patient's sense of self is greatly altered. However, when the nurse and patient are on equal footing, friends in a way, a patient can maintain at least some sense of control. Once these patients move into the Hospice Center setting, they fear they have lost their "home-field advantage," and it takes great skill and compassion on the part of the nurse to help them feel otherwise.

This is when you lean heavily on the Holy Spirit to guide your every word and deed, as there is no way humanly possible to know the patient as you would like to. The staff in a facility often enters the patient's and family's life when everyone and everything seems to be in crisis. Fear, anxiety, pain, shortness of breath, weakness, and sadness all roll into one and are often the reason for the admission in the first place. It is the nurse's primary responsibility to look past all the chaos regarding the family dynamics, putting the patient first and addressing every one of their needs as soon as possible, all the while appearing calm, tender, and in charge.

Thus it was with Sam on the day of admission. I believed one of the most important things I could do for Sam was to immediately make him feel safe and comfortable. Once I was able to address his symptoms and alleviate his fear and anxiety, Sam realized it was better for him to be in the Hospice Center than at home. That alone made life better for him and for Martha, who was feeling guilty about wanting him to be at the Hospice Center rather than at home while he was dying.

Sam settled in quickly, and as he did so, his anxiety level and fears decreased greatly. As is often the case in patients this close to death, once the symptoms of pain, fear, and anxiety are addressed, the patient is able to relax and be at peace for the first time in a long while. As it happened, Sam spent only four days with us. The hired caregivers remained faithful and continued to care for him at the Hospice Center as they had at home. I had the sacred honor of being with Sam and Martha as he took his final breath. Susan was with him as well.

Susan's first thought was to call Connie and let her know of Sam's death, as she had been so faithful and compassionate in her caring of him. After a few minutes, I heard Susan crying softly, and as she hung up the phone, she asked to speak with me. She wanted to tell me about the phone conversation she'd just had with Connie regarding Sam. Connie told Susan that as she was sitting at Sam's bedside at about 2:00 that morning, Sam had awakened suddenly and sat straight up. Pointing to a seemingly empty chair across the room, he looked at Connie and said in a clear, strong voice, "See that little girl over there, sitting in the chair? She is here to help me die." He then lay back down on his pillow and went to sleep.

As Susan related the conversation, her tears continued to fall, and I just knew there was more to the story than she had told me. You see, Susan's eleven-year-old niece Alice had died just over a year ago, and Susan often thought of her during her prayer time. Just two days before Sam's death, she prayed for Sam and asked God to help him die peacefully.

God honored Susan's prayer, offered in love, by sending a little Catholic girl to help an elderly Jewish man die in peace.

Alex

"I am ready to meet my Commander now"

Trudy Harris

Alex had been a lifelong navy man. He lived and breathed navy life and service to his God and country. He conducted his entire life with discipline and commitment. It was no different now.

Alex had inoperable cancer of the lung, and although at sixty-six he looked remarkably well, he was dying quickly. He accepted his terminal diagnosis, as I am sure he accepted everything in life, with strength and grace, dealing with every challenge with the stoicism and calm reflective of his naval discipline and his faith.

Alex's family was a navy family through and through. Sons had joined, just as their father and grandfather had done before them. In addition, as tough and disciplined as they all were, they admired, respected, and loved their father with great affection and without embarrassment. It was wonderful to see.

Taking turns with their wives and children, they helped to care for the father who had loved them all well and taught them to be committed Christian husbands, fathers, and navy men.

His wife, relieved now of some of Alex's day-to-day care, was able to offer her tender, loving presence to Alex in ways that were meaningful to both of them. Sitting quietly together on the patio, taking a short walk, or sharing morning and evening prayer meant everything to them. They loved each other deeply.

Each day, things got a little harder for Alex to do. Getting out of bed, bathing himself, even with help, and walking any distance took all of his energy now. Eating was difficult and began to take more and more out of him. Alex began to talk openly about going to heaven, to the God he had loved and served all of his life. "It will be time to meet my Commander soon," he said more than once, and he seemed to be preparing, on many levels, to do just that in the very near future.

A hurried call in the middle of the night sent me flying to their home at about 3:00 a.m. "He wants to have a shower and a shave *now*," his wife explained. "He wants to get dressed in his navy blues, and he wants us to help him." Apparently, Alex, in his many conversations with God, had gotten the clear message that it was time to go to his home in heaven and present himself to his Commander. There was no way to talk him into delaying this until morning. He wanted to do it now, and no amount of conversation was going to change his mind. Persuading his sons to take him into the shower, shave him, and dress him took enormous determination on Alex's part, but he did not waver, even for a moment. They gathered everything together as he directed, and the bathroom door closed behind him and his two sons.

When the door finally opened about thirty minutes later, Alex stood with his sons' assistance in his best navy dress blues, smiling from ear to ear. With Alex's encouragement, his sons helped him sit up straight in his king-sized bed, with pillows at his back and his officer's cap beside him. He then looked at all of them and smiled. "I am ready to meet my Commander now, whenever He is ready for me." There was not a shred of doubt in anyone's mind that when he did, God would say to him, "Welcome, My good and faithful servant. See what I have prepared for you from the beginning of time. You have loved Me well."

Alex died a few hours later, proudly surrounded by his family and loved ones. Dressed in the uniform of his beloved country, which he had served for a lifetime, he entered heaven.

I was reminded the entire time of the Scripture in which the centurion asks Jesus to heal his servant. The centurion tells Jesus that he too is a man under authority, and Jesus sees his great faith and rewards him. Alex saw himself as the centurion did, under authority, and ready to meet his Supreme Commander.

Dolly

"Heal the brokenhearted, bring comfort to those in pain"

Trudy Harris

Dolly was ninety-six years old, living out her last days in the Hospice Center, and dying ever so slowly of old age. She had been on her own since her husband's death decades earlier. She had no children and had outlived all of her friends and intimate family members. How long had it been since anyone had held Dolly, touched her, spent time with her, or listened to her? The Hospice staff took to her like jelly to bread, joking and talking with her often. They encouraged her to venture out of her room, to take a slow walk to the chapel in the center of the building, or to enjoy the sunshine in one of the many gardens. Each and every day they brought her any food she asked for, any special dessert, cup of tea, or soft drink, and all in all she was having a very sweet time in the remaining days of her life.

In Hospice work, you come to recognize God's hand in all things, often through the people who visit and the volunteers who devote their time to making the last days of a patient's life the best they can be. Through them, you see Christ's healing touch and recognize His voice.

One morning as I was walking from room to room, visiting patients and families, I saw Dolly all dressed up with gloves and purse and sitting in a corner nook, looking as if she were going someplace special. "Dolly," I said, "you look so pretty today. Are you going out?"

"I am going to have a massage this morning," she replied while pointing to the end of the corridor. (A massage therapist volunteers at the Hospice Center; the massages help with pain relief and make the patient feel better.)

"This is my first time," she said. "But I am not going to take any of my clothes off." She smiled demurely as she said this, and it was evident that a massage was a new experience for her. Just imagine the courage it took to have a massage for the first time at ninety-six years old—very adventuresome to say the least.

How wonderful that God would provide a healing touch in the form of a massage to an elderly woman who would soon be home with Him in heaven. The gentle hands of the therapist did wonders for Dolly that day, comforting her body, relieving it of aches and pains, but also comforting her heart. She told me later that she had found a friend in the therapist, who had spoken to her about God's love and His plans for her heavenly reward. I do not think she had spoken to anyone recently about God, and since she had been housebound for a long while, she probably had not been able to go to church either. Isn't it amazing how God presents Himself and His comfort to His children? Who would have thought of a massage? I don't think I would have. I believe this therapist was handpicked to comfort Dolly in all the ways she needed it most.

The next week I found Dolly again sitting in the same corner nook, ready to go somewhere special. This time, she was without her gloves and purse, and she seemed pleased to be going to the "healing lady" again. She longed to hear the words shared by the volunteer who heeded Christ's words telling the apostles and disciples to go out and heal the brokenhearted and to bring comfort to those in pain. As Dolly walked toward the massage room, she turned to me and smiled. "I think it will be better if I take my clothes off this time," she said with a wink. And I thought of the Scripture verse that tells us, "The Lord is the Spirit, and where the Spirit of the Lord is, there is freedom" (2 Cor. 3:17).

Freedom on a spiritual, emotional, and physical level is so desired as we approach our time of dying. We hope and pray that our patients experience this freedom so they, like Dolly, can "let go" of everything on a worldly plane and enter their heavenly home the way they entered the world—free, pure, and unencumbered. Dolly died a few weeks later, assured of God's love for her in ways she had not known about or understood before.

David

"Brave little soldier"

Ede Pearson Huston

David was a twelve-year-old African American who had leukemia. He lived in a very poor section of our town, with boarded-up, abandoned buildings and rampant drug activity. Sadly, David did not respond to any therapy he had received, and the children's hospital recommended him to our Hospice program. He lived at home with his primary caregiver—his mother—while his father was away in prison.

David was always concerned about his mother because she had a terrible time coping, not only with caring for him but also with the fact that she was going to lose him. David's concern for his mother was apparent to everyone who knew him. One day, while I was visiting him, he said to me, "Please don't tell anyone in the neighborhood that you're with Hospice, because they'll break in and look for drugs, and they'll hurt my mom." Here was David, dying of a childhood disease the doctors could not cure, all the while being more concerned for his mother's safety than for his own.

David, for sure, was a brave little soldier, trying to be so strong and far more mature than the twelve-year-old he was. David had been mature beyond his years for most of his life. On one of my visits, I brought him a stuffed teddy bear from my office, trying to bring him comfort in any way I could think of. David looked at me, laughing, and asked, "How old do you think I am?" He placed the bear at the foot of his bed. "I'm not a baby." I told him I would leave it here at his home and that one day he just might like having it. Little did I know that he was one step ahead of me and loved it.

David and I always had fun together. Many times, he would try to teach me how to play his video games. I could never get it. He would laugh and say, "You are so dumb that you can't catch on to that." He got the biggest kick out of the fact that he could play the games and I could not, and I think it was a good equalizer for him. In his life, David always had to be smarter than the rest, just to get by and take care of his own.

One day, as David began to decline, he said to me, "If I die, I know I'll go to heaven."

"Yes, you will," I responded.

David continued, "When I die, my mom can't be here alone, because she isn't going to handle this well." He asked me to promise him that when he told me to take him into the hospital, I would. "I'll know Jesus is ready for me. I want to go to the hospital to die, so my mom isn't alone and doesn't have a really hard time with this. Can you do that for me?" David asked.

"Yes," I said, "you let me know when you're ready to go, and I'll make that happen for you."

Where does this kind of courage come from? How can a child so young be so completely wrapped up in a parent's needs so as not to be concerned about his own?

Not long after that conversation, I went to see David. He said to me, "I want you to take me to the hospital now. I think I'm ready. I had a vision of Jesus last night, and He let me know that He's coming to get me. I want you to take me to the hospital so that Mom has some support, so you guys can help her when I die."

I immediately called an ambulance to take him to the hospital. Just as we were leaving, I asked David if he wanted to take anything with him to the hospital, anything he would like to hold on to.

He smiled at me. "Well, seeing as you brought me that teddy bear, why don't you give it to me and I'll take it with me."

David died two days later, just when he knew that Jesus was coming for him. He was at the hospital where he wanted to be, when the time was right. His mother was with him, as was the Hospice team and all the nurses who had gotten to know and love him so much. He saw all of us surrounding his bed, helping his mother as he entered heaven, just the way he asked us to. He was not frightened at all, either for his mother or for himself. Everything was in order, just as he hoped it would be.

That experience, although very sad, made me feel good too. We all knew where David was now, at peace, pain free, and in heaven. We had fulfilled his wishes, just as he asked, so that his mother was not alone. He was at peace.

Dorothy

"A goat named Daisy followed the horse into the room"

Bonnie Tingley

I was assigned to care for Dorothy, an independent woman in her early sixties who lived by herself with the animals she dearly loved. Breast cancer was quickly taking her life, despite the fact she had much more living to do. Before making my first visit to her home, I was cautioned about the bull that roamed freely in her fenced-in front yard. When I called ahead to confirm my first visit, she informed me the bull was friendly as long as I didn't show any fear. I quickly reminded myself about how much I love animals—but a bull, that was a bit much!

Reaching her home, I found a small white house with a beautiful yard wrapping around to the back of her long lot, surrounded by a chain-link fence. I didn't see any bull, so I quietly walked up the sidewalk, thanking the Lord for the good fortune He had bestowed on me. Suddenly, out of left field—literally—came a bull bouncing along like a frisky dog. I was greeted with a nudge and a big lick.

The worst seemed to be over. I had survived, and Dorothy was right—the bull was indeed friendly. Dorothy let me in with a big smile and said, "I see you have met Brutus!" Both of us laughed as she headed for her small family room with me in tow.

We began to talk. First and foremost, we discussed her physical needs and tweaked some of the medications she was taking, which would help her be more comfortable. Dorothy wanted to be able to do as much as she could, both inside the house and out, for as long as she could. As we were talking about her need for independence, the sliding glass door opened, and to my immense surprise, in walked a big white horse. Dorothy introduced me to Princess as the horse meandered into the room and laid her head on Dorothy's chest, nuzzling her with affection and familiarity. I must admit I was stunned, but a moment later, a goat named Daisy followed the horse into the family room. Dorothy said it was really hard to keep her beloved animals outside since she had become sick and unable to get outside to care for them. They just wanted to be near her. She also had an "inside dog," Tippy, who was always at her side.

Obviously, a great deal of attention was needed here, not only for Dorothy but for her animal friends as well. In the months that followed, we shared many exciting and entertaining visits. Dorothy's main concerns revolved around the future of her animals. Before long, her energy level began to decline sharply, and I worried more and more about Dorothy and her animals.

One day I arrived to find that a neighbor couple and their two children had moved in to lend a hand to Dorothy and her menagerie. I was reminded of when St. Paul spoke about caring for the widows and the orphans. This family was truly following Jesus's teaching to "love one another as I have loved you." They shared both the joys and the burdens of Dorothy's everyday life. I saw that they had been slowly taking over animal chores, cleaning the house, fixing her meals, and making life as nice for her as possible. Dorothy had complete trust in this couple and their children, and it seemed her "family" had grown for the better.

The animals were no longer allowed in the house, except for Tippy, who remained always at Dorothy's side. When the time came for Dorothy to settle into a hospital bed, Tippy remained either under the bed or on the floor right next to the bed at all times.

Dorothy and I discussed her spiritual needs. She said that she was peaceful with her approaching death and was confident that the Lord would take care of her. We made decisions about where her animals would go and who would care for them when she was gone. This brought her great peace.

Dorothy mentioned she had a sister who had not come to visit her for years. She and her sister were estranged because the sister did not like Dorothy's animals or approve of the way she lived. They were two very different people, and the estrangement was sad for both of them. She arrived the day before Dorothy died.

As Dorothy quickly approached the end of her life, she became more peaceful and accepting of her circumstances with every passing day because the young couple took such great care of her. Scripture tells us, "We are ambassadors for Christ, as if God were appealing through us" (2 Cor. 5:20). This family was doing just that. They had put her mind at ease about her wonderful animals, so she could let go without any stress. She knew her Lord well and felt safe in His care and in the care of those He had sent to her.

One fall morning, I received an early call telling me that Dorothy had died quietly during the night. As I entered the house, Dorothy's sister greeted me somewhat formally.

I proceeded to make the necessary calls to her physician, the Hospice team, the funeral home that would carry out her burial wishes, and her church, which had supported her so well. I offered my condolences to her sister.

Her sister took me aside and informed me that she had removed Dorothy's caregivers from the home without explanation; I was then ushered promptly to the front door in the same way.

Later that afternoon, I received a call from Dorothy's young friends, the ones who had surrounded her with so much love and had reflected the heart of Jesus to her. They said they had sat up with Dorothy all night and that she had experienced a very sweet and gentle death. The couple felt honored to have been able to give Dorothy peace of mind, comfort, and reassurance. I know how thankful Dorothy was for them, for the gift of being able to remain in her own home, to have her animals well cared for, and to be in charge of her own life until the end.

Henry

"I felt the Holy Spirit nudge me in a way I had never experienced before"

Trudy Harris

Henry was one of the sweetest and gentlest Italian men I had ever met. He had lost his wife of many years and was now living alone in a part of town that named every street after a World War II general or battle. He had a lovely little house with a sitting room in the front and a stoop in the back that overlooked the grapevines he tended with great care. Henry had only one son, who lived a good distance away but was very committed to and concerned with his father's health and welfare. This son had inherited many of his father's kind and gentle ways and held his dad in great esteem.

Henry was declining slowly but surely, seldom complaining and always receptive to any suggestion or assistance I offered. He was clearly someone who had led a God-centered life, thinking of others, not drawing attention to himself, anxiously waiting to go home to the God whom he knew loved him. I asked myself, How and where was Henry to spend his last days? Should he stay at home with assistance from neighbors and friends or travel to his son's home, where he would be loved and cared for but where he had no friends?

Nurses often develop a close kinship with those in their care, and so it was with Henry and me. He was the kind of person for whom you wanted to do as much as possible. You wanted him to be comfortable and safe at all times, to have no fears. You wanted only the best for him and to see that he returned to his Creator safe and sound.

During this time, I had to be away from Henry for about two weeks, as my family was going on vacation. I asked my dear friend and fellow Hospice nurse Jackie to visit and care for Henry in my absence. Jackie did it well and loved Henry as much as I did, and she announced upon my return that she planned to continue to visit him even though he was not her patient. My Irish got the better of me for a moment, and the old issues of territory and jealousy reared their ugly heads. I had to ask myself if I was more concerned about controlling things and having my own way or about what was best for Henry. It is in times like these that we recognize God's hand refining our souls and teaching us how to be more like Him—but it is never easy. Jackie and I decided that we would both be Henry's nurses, which was a well-kept secret from our supervisor, who would not have approved of the arrangement.

After a few months passed, the time for Henry to go on to God began to draw near. We needed to have a discussion about where Henry would die, and his son, with whom I was in regular contact, was coming to town to talk about it all. I asked Jackie to accompany me when visiting Henry and his son, since she cared about him as much as I did.

To say that this was a difficult time in Jackie's life is an enormous understatement. Newly divorced after twenty-five years of marriage to a man she dearly loved, Jackie was suffering terribly. Her sense of abandonment and loneliness affected every aspect of her daily living, and she was seeking God's presence in her life and was hungry to know that He loved and cared for her. I mention this here only to illustrate the importance of listening to and obeying the Holy Spirit's whisperings when He is directing you, which was what I was about to experience.

We met with Henry and his son in the sitting room of his home and reviewed all the options of care open to him. While he hated to leave his home with all its memories and the few friends he still had there, he decided he would go with his son and his family and remain with them until God called him home. Henry was both happy and sad about the decision. Happy that he would be with his son where he knew he would be cared for and safe. Sad that he was leaving so much behind. But he knew his decision was best for everyone.

When we were finished talking and Jackie and I were getting ready to leave, I felt the Holy Spirit quietly nudge me in a way I had never experienced before. The Spirit allowed me to understand clearly that I was to leave the room and walk outside. I did so, as if I'd heard an audible voice directing me, and I seated myself on the stoop in the outside garden, leaving Jackie with Henry's son. After twenty or thirty minutes had passed, I returned inside the house to speak to Henry again, to tell him good-bye and to thank his son for loving his father so well. Henry's son promised to stay in touch regarding his dad's well-being, which he did faithfully.

When we got into the car, Jackie shared with me the conversation she'd had with Henry's son. He had, in the tenderest and gentlest way, told her just how good she was, how kind, how perfect she was for the job of ministering to the dying, and how grateful he was to her for all of the love and support she had given to his father. Hugging her, he told her that he loved her in such a way that Jackie knew the words were not his. It was as though Jesus Himself was loving and reassuring her—no one else could possibly know how much that would mean to her right now.

"How did you know to leave the room?" she asked. "What made you go outside and leave me in there alone?" I explained to her the experience I'd had of the Holy Spirit's clear prompting. We spoke about how much is lost when we do not recognize God's voice or do not choose to hear and obey. It was more than evident to me that day that Jesus Himself wanted to comfort and reassure Jackie and let her know that she was loved and safe in His care. He did just that through this lovely, gentle son and the experience of his own father's death. I stayed in close touch with Henry's son, and when Henry died, I received a beautiful letter letting Jackie and me know that his dad was now safely in heaven.

Mr. D.

"There must be something nice about him that I don't know about"

Trudy Harris

In the early years of Hospice care in our community, we were housed in any little office or space that a "good Samaritan" donated to us. Sometimes it was a space beneath a stairwell, sometimes two or three tiny rooms with grade-school desks donated by a friend. We always made certain—because the understanding of Hospice care was new—that our sign out front was a welcoming one. We felt strongly that it should be inviting enough to make people feel as if they could stop in and simply ask questions about a loved one or perhaps just sit and share a story.

One such morning, a mailman named John stopped in. He told us that he had been delivering mail to a "mean old guy, Mr. D.," for years. Never a kind word had come out of Mr. D.'s mouth, never a thank-you, never a mention of the thoughtfulness of the mailman when on rainy days the mail arrived safe and dry within the screen door. "Never a smile, and more often than not, the old man would give a grumbling comment or complaint about the smallest things," the mailman said. Mr. D. sure sounded hard to like, and John could not hide his feelings.

Years passed, and the mailman realized that he had been seeing Mr. D. less and less often. And then, sometimes for a long stretch, he did not see him at all. Mr. D. should not have been surprised to know that no one had asked about him, that no one mentioned him or wondered where or how he was. No, Mr. D. had not been a friend to anyone, and now (not surprisingly) no one cared about him.

But wait, all of a sudden John noticed that nice people were stopping by with a friendly word or wave. Often he would see them coming and going as he made his deliveries. And sometimes in the evening, as he was going home, he would see them again, happily visiting Mr. D. at a late hour. Who were they? he wondered. What were they doing there and why did they all seem so nice?

John told me that one day his curiosity got the better of him, so he asked a neighbor of Mr. D.'s what was happening. "He's dying," said the lady next door, "and all those people you see coming and going work for Hospice. They are nurses and doctors and volunteers who bring him food and spend time with him. They're taking care of him until he dies."

John said that he was deeply moved by what the neighbor had shared with him. He wondered why, in all the years he had been delivering Mr. D.'s mail, he had not recognized even one nice thing about him that others might be seeing now. *There must be something nice about him that I don't know about*, he thought.

He decided to ring the doorbell one morning and then asked the Hospice volunteer if he could give the mail to Mr. D. personally. She invited him into the house. To John's surprise, Mr. D. seemed genuinely happy to see him and asked him if he could stay awhile. "I can only stop for a minute today, because I have to finish my route," John said, but he asked Mr. D. if he could stop by to check on him on his way home sometimes. This was the beginning of a very tender and compassionate friendship—one that surprised them both.

The mailman told Mr. D. that although he was a faithful churchgoer and believed in the Lord with all of his heart, he did not feel he had done what Jesus asked him to do. Clearly, Jesus had told His followers, "Blessed are the merciful, for they will be shown mercy" (Matt. 5:7). He felt he had hardened his heart to Mr. D. and had written him off early in his service to him. He had been given many opportunities over the years to make a difference in Mr. D.'s life but had allowed his judgments to cloud his behavior toward him. He felt great remorse now for having done so and tried hard to make up for lost time. They spoke about this for a long time, and Mr. D. just listened. He seemed to understand and did not respond in any way; he simply smiled.

John said he was happy that God had allowed him to get to know Mr. D. in the final months of his life. He found him to be a very nice man and interesting to talk to. He discovered Mr. D. had a unique story all his own, as most people do when you get to know them. Mr. D. confided to him one day while they were visiting that he had lost, in two separate tragedies, everyone in his entire family. He said he had been too sad to speak to anyone about it and could not find the words to express his sorrow. He found it easier to shut himself off from the world and could not even find a way to talk to God anymore.

His newfound friendship with John was a gift for him and a way to get back in touch with God, whom he knew had somehow always been with him. John and Mr. D. marveled at the way God could intervene in two very different lives and heal each of their wounds. God always touches both sides of the coin, so to speak, when dealing with His children. I have always found it a good thing to watch closely when He is teaching someone whom I think needs a lesson, to see what it is He is teaching me as well. I have learned some important lessons when I have left myself open to understanding something that I was not looking to learn. God never ceases to surprise us if we are open to learning to love as He does.

Shortly after Mr. D.'s death, John came into the Hospice office. He told me it was the smiles he had seen on the faces of the Hospice nurses and volunteers when they visited Mr. D. that made him curious. It was the constancy of the care he saw arriving all day and late into the evening that made him wonder if he had misjudged Mr. D. in some way. He was grateful to God to be able to make up for lost time and to have learned the lesson that Jesus taught us when he said that loving people who love you is easy. But He asks us to love as His heavenly Father does, perfectly.

The mailman was a faithful friend and visitor to Mr. D. until the day he died. He attended his funeral as well, along with the Hospice staff and volunteers who had cared for him. I know; I saw him there.

Karla

"It is not good for man to be alone"

Trudy Harris

Karla was a woman in her late forties, in love with life, her family, and most of all her husband, David. When we first met, she was living and dying with a diagnosis of ovarian cancer, end stage. She was fighting with every breath in her to stay alive, to love deeply, and to protect all those around her. She did not want to die; she simply was not ready. Everyone responds to illness differently. Some people want to have loved ones and friends around them, to be touched, hugged, kissed, and fussed over. Some, on the other hand, pull inward and wish to remain somewhat separate from everyone else and to handle things in their own way. Karla loved to be near the people she loved.

Karla's husband adored her, but as is often the case, he did not know how to express his love the way he always had, openly and with a great sense of fun and affection. His aloofness, or in his mind, his "carefulness," around Karla made her feel so alone that she could hardly bear it. The intimacy they had shared in the past was no longer there. Her husband was afraid of touching her for fear of causing her pain so that Karla was left to feel sad, alone, and unable to express herself. David, too, experienced a great sense of loss, but he could not find the words to tell Karla how he felt. He was afraid that it would sound too selfish. The playfulness that had enriched their lives for as long as either of them could remember was gone now, and the pain it caused was huge.

Each time I visited Karla, I sensed an enormous sadness in her, separate from her physical needs of pain control and symptom management. Family was all around her—church friends, Hospice sitters, and volunteers were coming and going day and night. The house was never quiet. However, Karla reflected an aloneness that reminded me of the night Jesus spent in the Garden of Gethsemane. Yes, He wanted His friends to stay awake with Him, but at a distance. He longed to communicate with His Father and to talk to Him about all that lay ahead. Karla, too, was grateful for the friends who were helping in her home, but she needed them to be at a distance from her. She longed to be alone with her husband. With the way things were now, this was not possible.

During one of my visits with Karla, I asked everyone except David to leave the living room, where her hospital bed was placed, so that we could speak in private. I took Karla's hands in mine; I touched my heart and my head and said to her, "Tell me what is going on in here and up here."

Karla looked at me and immediately began to cry. "I feel so alone right now," she said. "I know that sounds foolish, because there are so many people here all day long with me, but it's just not the same. David and I have no privacy anymore. Someone is always around, and we are never *truly* alone. It is so hard."

I waited for a long time as Karla cried deeply, which in her weakened state left her exhausted. "I miss him so much," she said as she turned and looked at David. "He sleeps all alone in our bedroom. I know he loves me, but he's afraid to touch me, and the days of holding each other seem to be over sooner than they should be." David quietly reached for Karla as she spoke, and she nestled her face into his shoulder as he held her tight. They remained that way for a long while.

When God created man and woman, He knew of the healing, wholeness, and intimacy He intended to be experienced by His children through the sacrament of marriage. In the inevitable joys and sorrows of life, He wanted them to be comforted by one another, and in doing so, to experience Him. Now when Karla needed her husband's love more than ever, and he hers, they were not sharing that gift which God had given to them. I quickly begged the Holy Spirit for some answers.

"How about some new rules for this house?" I asked. "How about putting up room dividers here in the living room, separating it from the rest of the house? In addition, after a certain hour of your choosing, no one can come into this space without your permission. For all intents and purposes, this is your space and no one else's from now on." Karla smiled for the first time in a long, long time. "What would you think if I got another hospital bed, same size as yours, and we tie them together and make it up as a king-sized bed so you and David can sleep together from now on?" Karla was enthusiastic, as was David, and she explained to him exactly where she wanted everything and how she wanted it to look. Linens, quilts, pillows, and every other detail were discussed, and I do not know who was more thrilled with this new arrangement—David or Karla.

On my next visit to their home, the dividers were firmly in place; their king-sized hospital bed was beautifully set up, and it looked for all the world like their own master bedroom. Everyone in the house knew and respected the new rules. It was as happy a place as it could possibly be from that day forward.

Karla continued to decline, but I never again visited her that she and her husband were not together, sitting close to each other, reading, touching, and kissing. When God said, "It is not good for man to be alone," this is what He meant. The healing touch of affirmation remains an important reality in all of our lives until the very end. Until Karla took her last breath in their quiet space, she and David were together.

When it was time for her to go, she left her husband's arms and moved gently into God's. Never has someone better understood that where love is, that's where God is present, than Karla and David.

Gerald and Mary

"Walk on into heaven now, Jesus is waiting for you"

Trudy Harris

Gerald and Mary were an older couple and neighbors of ours whom we saw on occasion. They died just a few months apart. Mary had been ill for a long time with cancer of the lung, but you could not find a stronger and more determined woman anywhere. She and Gerald were both professionals and successful in their individual careers. I did not know about their belief systems, as they were very private people, but learned of them close to the end of their lives.

Mary was a pragmatist; she saw things clearly as they were rather than through rose-colored glasses. She took her diagnosis and her prognosis in stride. She knew that in the end, she would not be able to beat this particular challenge as she had been able to do with most others throughout her life.

Mary wanted to ensure that Gerald, her husband of many years, would be safe and well cared for after her death. She, in truth, was far more ill than he was, and had many more life-threatening challenges, but it was Gerald who came into the Hospice program first. He had suffered for years with several chronic conditions that by now had taken their toll on him, and she saw that he was declining daily. She was determined that she would, as long as she could, see to his care, as she knew in her heart that he needed her now more than ever. She would see to her own care after he no longer needed her.

Gerald, knowing that time was growing short, held a huge celebration of their lives at the country club near his home. He invited everyone whose lives had significantly touched theirs and vice versa. Those who attended the celebration came from every walk of life, which included the gardener, the waiter at the club, neighbors and friends, and Dr. Browning, his physician, who could be found at his home on many a late-night visit. The gathering itself created a portrait of Gerald and Mary's lives and wordlessly showed how they had lived.

Gerald was generous by nature and had often helped people in need, especially when no one was looking. He simply saw a need and tended to it quickly. Gerald never drew any attention to himself for his good works, which reminded me of how often Jesus spoke of such things in Scripture. Gerald, I know, went into his prayer closet many times a day, and there, seen only by his heavenly Father, he came to understand all that his heavenly Father wanted him to.

He and Mary had visited me at the Hospice Center and told me of their desire to leave a gift to our program in their will. They loved the work that Hospice did and had seen many of their friends benefit from it. Their generosity enabled our Hospice program to renovate a large wing of the city hospital and to prepare it for the care and comfort of eighteen dying patients. After Mary and Gerald's deaths, the Hospice wing was named in their honor.

You would have to be in their home for only a moment to recognize how devoted Mary was to Gerald. She anticipated his every want and need and would see to his comfort all day long. It was through sheer grit and determination that Mary was able to do even the simplest of tasks for him due to her own illness. It was that determination and grit that allowed her to outlive him, something that her physicians and everyone close to them could never have anticipated. In the last months of their lives, they often spent quiet time together on their beautiful patio with friends stopping by, day and night.

Gerald and I spent many quiet afternoons discussing God's plan for him and Mary. He admitted to me that he simply trusted their care to His will. His thoughts did not so much reflect a resignation as it did a trust in the God he knew loved them both.

One afternoon while on my way home from work, Gerald's Hospice nurse called and asked me to stop by their house and visit with him. She had seen him earlier in the day and had the feeling that his time was very short. Since they lived only a few doors away from me, I stopped by within minutes of her call.

As I entered their home, I saw Gerald resting quietly on the sofa in the family room, Mary just a few steps away, in the kitchen. Kneeling down beside him on the floor and sensing clearly that he was about to die, I beckoned to Mary to come and join us. "Gerald," I said to him, "God is getting ready to take you into heaven now. Are you ready?"

Nodding his head ever so slowly, he replied, "Okay, okay."

"Mary is right here sitting with you now," I said as she patted his arm and kissed his forehead. "Walk on into heaven now, Jesus is waiting for you, you will see Him in just a minute."

Mary spoke a few gentle words to him, and with that, Gerald took his last breath. Mary was speechless. She said she never dreamed that dying could be so peaceful. She asked me if it was always that way, thinking, I am sure, of her own future. I reassured her that God loves us all deeply, and that He always wants us to come home to Him in safety and in peace. I do not think God was ever more present to Mary than in that very moment, and she simply smiled.

In the days following Gerald's death, Mary and I had many opportunities to share how happy she was that he was no longer suffering, and how grateful she was to see him die so beautifully. She explained to me that it was a great gift for her to have witnessed how gently death came for her husband, and if she had ever been fearful, she no longer was. The moment seemed very holy to her.

Mary died a few months later in her sleep, having loved her husband well. God gave her a profoundly beautiful understanding of His presence and love through Gerald's death, and I am certain He was with her as she entered heaven.

Mr. Winters

"Your paperwork is finished, there is nothing left to be done"

Cookie Schnier

The moments I treasured most during my time at the Hospice Center were the initial walks down the dark corridor as I arrived early each morning. I would stop at each room and look in on the patients and family members as I made my way to the nurses' station to begin my day.

"How is everything with you this morning?" I would ask. One morning, Mr. Winters, who was to be discharged to his home in about a week, summoned me to come closer to his bed. "I had a nightmare last night," he said to me. "I couldn't sleep. I dreamed I was in a place that had two tall iron fences, one in front of the other. Through the fences, I could clearly see many people on the other side that I knew had already died. They kept looking at me but didn't say a word. I managed to get the first gate opened, and when I got into the space between the first and the second gate, the first gate closed behind me quickly and I was completely trapped. I had nothing, no food, no water, and nothing to keep me warm. I started calling and calling loudly for someone to help me, but none of those people could hear me. A strange-looking man appeared in front of me. He looked at me carefully and said, 'You need to do your paperwork first,' and then he simply went away. It's a terrible dream as I am completely trapped and I have no way to get out and no one to help me."

I sat down on the chair beside his bed and listened very carefully to him as he related this nightmare to me. He seemed relieved just to have someone to tell about it, and when he was finished, he laid his head back onto his pillow, exhausted, and closed his eyes. "We'll talk later, when you're rested," I said to him as I left the room to continue my morning rounds of visiting other patients.

Later in the morning, I went back to visit Mr. Winters again, and we discussed the bad dream he had told me about earlier in the day. "Do you think this means something?" he asked me.

"Well, yes, I think it does," I said. "I believe you've been given a heads-up, if you will, that your time on earth is coming to a close and that you still have work to do to prepare yourself for your next life with your Creator."

"How am I supposed to do that?" he asked me. "I'm going home soon, you know, one day next week for sure."

"Don't worry about next week," I said to him. "Right now you need to patch the holes that seem to be in your soul. God sends us messages in unlikely ways sometimes. This is one of those times. You need to pay attention now. You are blessed to be given this extra time and a chance to make everything right. This is a warning, and you need to get busy and make certain that everything is right between you and others and with your Creator. Open your heart to God, and together with Him start fixing what is unresolved in your life. Whatever is not resolved between you and your family or friends and whatever is not settled between you and God, work on that now. Ask Him to show you what you need to do, and He'll help you, I promise." Mr. Winters remained quiet the whole time I was speaking, looking at me intently and taking in every word I said.

Every day for the rest of the week, Mr. Winters would sadly say to me each morning, "I had that nightmare again last night. It's terrible." Then he would repeat it exactly, word for word, never changing any detail of it, as if it was etched in his mind and heart completely. Each day, I would prayerfully encourage him to ask God to help him resolve everything that needed his attention, so that he could go home to Him in peace. It was evident to me that he was working on it in earnest, and so badly wanted it resolved.

One morning as I made my usual rounds, I stood in his doorway, trying to decide if he was asleep or awake. If he was sleeping, I did not want to disturb him, but when he sensed my presence, he turned to me and smiled. "Last night, the man came to me in my dream again. He said to me, 'Your paperwork is now finished, there is nothing left to be done.'" With that, he peacefully rolled over, closed his eyes, and fell asleep. He seemed relieved that his paperwork and all that it entailed had been completed, and now his heart could truly be at rest. During the next few days, Mr. Winters continued to be content and sleeping peacefully every time I stopped by to check on him. The day before Mr. Winters was to go home, he died in his sleep. His paperwork was completed, and he had now received his eternal reward, just as God wanted him to.

The Scriptures reflect many instances throughout history of God's messengers coming to earth to warn, to direct, and to enlighten His people. Joseph was warned by the angel to take Mary and Jesus into Egypt. Mary was told by the angel Gabriel that she was to be the mother of Jesus, and Jacob's son Joseph knew, through a dream, that he would one day rule over his brothers. God enlightens our minds and hearts today, in the very same ways. He stays with us until the end of our lives, wanting us to come home to Him for all eternity.

Luke

"Oh God, I can't go now, I can't go now"

Jackie Aquino

Luke's mom was in her early thirties and all alone in the world. Her husband and one of her sons were in prison; she had no extended family support to speak of and little education. Life with all of its heartaches had left her frightened, defensive, and terribly isolated. And now, beyond all comprehension, her beloved ten-year-old son, Luke, was dying of leukemia. It is at times like this that as a nurse and as a human being, I ask God, "Why?"

I knew on my first visit to the tiny apartment they lived in that Luke was the "man of the house." He was mature far beyond his ten years and spent a great deal of time protecting and explaining his mother to me. There was no phone, little furniture, an empty refrigerator, and a downstairs neighbor who helped out whenever she could.

With a diagnosis of leukemia and his experience of multiple hospital stays, Luke had seen up close the deaths of many of his peers who had died of the same disease that would soon take his young life. Even though the doctors and nurses caring for him pulled out all the stops to stave off the inevitable, it was not meant to be. Luke was going to die.

How was his mother to keep it all together? She needed to work but also needed to be with this young son, who was as brave as anyone I had ever known. I kept a close eye on the refrigerator and its contents and stopped at the store many times before a visit. As I headed to the refrigerator each time, Luke would say, "That's all right, we have plenty of food, thank you. I am never hungry." And even though the refrigerator was empty each time I looked, this denial was the only way Luke could protect his mother from the judgments of others, which I'm sure he had grown accustomed to hearing.

Think about "love in action" and what it really means. You see this mother, trying against all odds to care for her son, and this ten-year-old dying bravely and at the same time in charge of everything. The love and concern Luke exhibited for her were amazing to see, and it made me often stop and wonder if I loved as unselfishly as he did.

The days ticked by slowly; Luke was beginning to die, and he knew it. He told me one day while I was visiting that he had tried to be a good boy but sometimes was not. "I don't think I'm going to go to heaven," he said. "I didn't do right sometimes."

Looking at the cross on the wall, I said to him, "I've heard that you've been a very brave boy and that Jesus wants you to be in heaven with Him when it is time." I told him that when Jesus died on that cross, the gates of heaven opened for everyone who loved Him and believed in Him.

Luke seemed comforted by our talk, but I sensed that he wanted to say more. I waited. Finally, Luke looked up at me with big brown eyes brimming with tears and said, "Sometimes Jesus comes for me. He tells me He wants me to come with Him, but I tell Him, I can't go yet, not yet."

As Luke declined more and more each day, he could often be heard saying quietly, "Oh God, I can't go now, I can't go now."

One afternoon while I was visiting, I explained to his mother that Luke was ready to die but that he could not go without her permission. He needed the assurance that she would be all right when he went to heaven and that she would see him later. She would have to say these words to him, I told her, and let him know that the next time Jesus came for him, it was all right for him to go.

Permission to let go is often the only thing keeping a person from leaving peacefully when the time is right. Loved ones who are dying often have to be reassured that everyone will be "okay," and Luke certainly needed this reassurance.

One cannot even begin to imagine the pain to a mother's heart when a nurse, whose own son was not dying, tells her that she should give her son permission to leave her and go on to Jesus. She was furious, frightened, and heartbroken all at once, and I left her in tears. She thought about all I had said to her and called me later that evening. She had spoken to Luke in the afternoon and had assured him that she would be okay and that the next time Jesus came for him, he could go with Him and she would be fine.

A few evenings later, while she was sitting on his bed and holding him, she heard him say, "Mommy, I see Jesus now and I want to go with Him." With that, he closed his eyes and died.

She called me years later to tell me about all the good things she had accomplished with her life. She had gone back to school after Luke died and had gotten her GED. She then graduated from college and became a certified nursing assistant. She was a very happy and settled person. She told me that I was the only white person she had ever really known and yet I was the one who understood her best. I felt equally honored and blessed to have known her and her wonderful son Luke. They were both treasures in God's eyes.

Matt

"This angel man comes and sits on my bed"

Trudy Harris

Matt was a sixty-year-old man who had lived a very full life. He was diagnosed with a malignant tumor of the brain and was now being cared for at home by his wife and son. He often sat up in bed when I visited and shared with me the kind of work he had done during his lifetime and how much he enjoyed it. The fact that he had worked hard and been able to provide for his family meant everything to him.

Matt had another son, with whom he had not been on good terms over the years. This hurt Matt a great deal, but he was unsure what to do about it. Matt was in a quiet, restful time of his life when I first met him, neither immediately dying nor planning anything in the future. We spoke easily about many things as his wife busied herself preparing his meals and looking out for his comfort. She was a quiet soul, not given to a great deal of conversation, with a sweet way about her and a sense of humor that Matt enjoyed.

During one of my visits, Matt asked me to sit down. He had something he wanted to tell me about. He had been having an experience that he both liked and could not quite understand. "Trudy," he said to me, "this angel man comes and sits on my bed, and he just smiles at me. He's tall with blond hair and white robes, and he's very beautiful." I kidded with him when he described the angel as both beautiful and male at the same time. Looking away for a moment and then back to me, he smiled and said, "Oh yes, he is a man and he is very beautiful."

"Do you feel badly when you see him?" I asked.

"Oh no," he said, "I only feel badly when he goes away."

Matt spoke about the fact that the angel came to visit him often. And as always, when people share these types of experiences, he did so with a naturalness that defies understanding. You would expect lots of dramatics when these things occur, but that is never the case. People simply share, as Matt was now doing, with no real awe expressed; in fact, they often sound more natural in their telling than other things they speak about going on around them.

After a few months, Matt began to rapidly decline, and for three straight days he slept, eating nothing and not responding in any way. When I visited him early in the morning on the fourth day, I found him awake and responsive. "Where have you been, Matt?" I said to him.

"Oh, I've been talking to God," he answered naturally. He seemed comfortable and at peace with himself, and it shocked his wife and son when he asked to see the son he had not been with in a long while. He wanted him to come as soon as possible.

Over the many years of caring for dying patients, I saw more often than not this quiet reverie of time during which I truly believe God converses with the soul He is drawing home. It seems during this time that the person develops an insight, a new way of looking at things, that gives them great new understanding and peace. Many times following this reverie, the person will ask to see someone special from whom they have been separated. A desire to heal some wound or forgive some wrong or make things right seems to take hold of the person; it is as if there is a mind shift, or maybe a shift in the soul, so to speak. This was obviously happening with Matt now. He asked to see the son he had always loved but from whom he was estranged. His son came immediately.

So often in life God draws our minds and hearts back to the lessons He taught us through the Gospels two thousand years ago. We find ourselves experiencing a true-life story today through which He shows us some insight He wants us to understand and make our own. The prodigal son story, with the loving father going to meet the son who left home, reminds us of God's enormous love and His desire to have us safely home with Him. The story, in this instance, was lost on no one.

Some people say they do not read the Scriptures today because they already know the story. I feel so badly for them. They do not allow God to show them the full meaning of the Gospel stories and how they apply to their own lives. The Bible is the "living" Word of God and is speaking to us in new and meaningful ways all the time if only we will listen.

Matt and his son spent hours together for the first time in many, many years. And Matt died having understood his son's love for him in a way he did not know before, and his son understood that his father had never stopped loving him.

Some twenty years later that son waited with his wife outside a hospital conference room where I was speaking. He called me by name as I stepped out of the building, and it took no time at all for me to remember his dad and mom and his family story. He said he wanted to see me again after all those years and brought a picture of himself to remind me of who he was at the time I met him. There was no need. I remembered him well. We were like friends meeting again after a very long time as we hugged each other and reminisced about how God works in all of our lives every day.

Cara

"I feel so sorry for him; he is so sad"

Trudy Harris

Cara was only forty-two years old, divorced, with an eighteen-year-old daughter who had many problems. Cara had been diagnosed two years earlier with ovarian cancer, which had now spread throughout her abdomen. She had been under the care of a well-known and dedicated oncologist, Dr. Marc, at a large medical center in our community.

This woman was braver than anyone I had ever met before. Her concern was never for herself but for her daughter, whose father had not been involved with her for years and from whom she had never received any loving support. Cara's pain and the associated symptoms of her disease would have stopped almost anyone else in their tracks, but not her.

Cara was deeply involved in her faith and her church, and in turn she had many visitors who would stop by, bringing their guitars with them and singing to her. Her dedication to the church choir had always been an important part of her life, and it meant everything to her that the choir members would spend this meaningful time with her now. The Sisters of St. Joseph, an order of nuns at her parish, took turns staying with Cara, driving her to appointments and bringing her favorite foods and treats to eat. The most important thing they did for Cara was to bring Holy Communion to her each week, and they prayed with her often.

Cara's pain was severe, and she was on heavy doses of narcotics in an effort to relieve her symptoms and give her comfort. Pain control and management of symptoms are important to the well-being and comfort of a terminally ill patient, and it occurred to me that Cara's pain was not as well-controlled as it should have been, so I asked her about it. There was some hesitancy on her part in answering me right away, and I came to the conclusion that her medications needed to be handled differently. We decided that they would no longer be out in the open and henceforth under lock and key, with only Cara's mother dispensing them.

A great deal of secrecy exists in families where the use and misuse of drugs takes place. Cara was trying hard to speak well of her daughter and not allow us to see what was more than evident. Enabling is a common problem in instances such as this, and it gets its hooks in family life in a most insidious way. First, the drug use is denied, then it is excused, then it is explained away, and finally it has to be faced and dealt with—which is the hardest part of all.

Cara's heart was very heavy, not only because of her own illness, which was more than enough to stress about, but also because she was concerned about leaving her daughter. She was dealing not only with her impending death but with her daughter's drug use and long-term welfare as well. In order for Cara to die well, a plan had to be in place for her daughter's future. Nothing less would do. Many professional friends, clergy, and family members took a serious part in addressing this need, and together they devised a plan to make it happen. Once Cara died, her daughter would be given the opportunity to get her life in order by going to a place for treatment of her drug problems. There was no way to make this happen before Cara died, as it was all-important for her daughter to stay with her as long as she could.

Often when I visited, I would get up on the bed with Cara and just hold her. As strange as that might sound, it was the most natural thing to do, and it would bring such tender comfort to her. By this time, I had developed very close ties with Cara, almost like sisters, and I would do for her exactly what a sister would do under such circumstances. And Cara and I would pray quietly together. She was the most trusting of all souls, and she would often cry through her prayers as she begged God to help her daughter find her way. She prayed, almost like a child, and I am certain that God's heart was listening closely to her pleas.

Time was running out quickly for Cara. Her oncologist was deeply saddened that he could not make her well. "I want you to make an appointment with Dr. Marc for me," Cara said. "I want to go and tell him how grateful I am for all that he has done for me over the years, and for always being kind to me." I called Dr. Marc's office to make an appointment, explaining carefully the purpose of Cara's visit. Under great strain, effort, pain, and determination on Cara's part, I took her to see her doctor. We waited in the examining room for a long time for him to arrive, and when he finally entered the room, I could read the sadness and deep pain on his face. Looking at Cara, he said, "I just don't understand how you are still here; you've been so good through all of this. How are you holding on?"

"I just don't know how to let go," Cara replied. She continued on, telling him how grateful she was to him for being her doctor and for caring about her so much. At this point, it was obvious that Dr. Marc could simply no longer bear it, and he hastily backed out of the room without another word, head down, attempting to control his emotions.

I turned to Cara, and the heartache on her face was stunning. "I feel so sorry for him. He couldn't say anything to me at all," she said. "He is so sad."

At that point, I left Cara for a moment and stepped into Dr. Marc's office, only to find him with his face in his hands, sobbing. This highly skilled, committed, compassionate oncologist found the bravery and gratitude of Cara too painful to bear. I thought of how much more healing it would have been for both of them if only he had been able to express to her what he was feeling as well. Shared tears, in any circumstance, allow for a genuine expression of heartfelt emotions, allowing people to be "real" with one another and to find healing.

There is never real closure for physicians without some exchange of true feelings. So often, when they cannot cure their patients, they are bereft of the words that one ordinarily expects to be expressed in the face of such sorrow. Dr. Marc and Cara were the same age, and he could not fathom losing a patient so young. Although he had done everything humanly possible for her, I am sure he felt, in some way, that he had let her down.

God's presence was everywhere in Cara's life, in the doctor that cared for her for two years, in the volunteers who visited her often, in the Sisters of St. Joseph who loved her so well. Cara herself reflected Christ's presence in all that she did for others, even in the face of her own impending death. She died two weeks later, knowing that as much as she loved her daughter, God loved her even more. He would see to it that her daughter received the care she needed through those He put around her, until she was well again. His eyes and ears, His hands and heart would simply be others standing in His place.

James

"Are you finished now? I love you too"

Dianne Rigby

"Okay, team, I have our list of new patients," the nursing supervisor announced. "Our first one has expressed loudly that he does not care who comes to take care of him as long as they are not Christian. He does not want to hear anything about Jesus!" Immediately I thought, *I'll take him! Can I have this patient?*

From the moment I arrived for my first visit, I was impressed by James's extraordinary intelligence and distinguished good looks. This gentleman was a world-renowned chess player, a doctor of philosophy, and a man of much accomplishment. He also was quick to inform me that the gods he worshipped were time and knowledge, and I would listen to him intently as he began to share his world with me.

I remember always making sure that my cross ring and necklace were facing outward perfectly before entering his home and being sure not to say a word about Jesus! We would sit around this little table while I listened to him talk about his big world that, ironically, had become so small now. The world, as this sixty-eight-year-old man dying of mesothelioma had known it, was changing rapidly for him. James made it clear to me that he did not love the God I serve, but I knew without any doubt that my God loved him. I had a good feeling that He was going to bless us both, despite our differences, in ways that we just could not yet comprehend.

Over the next six months, our friendship grew. I knew in my heart that God was speaking to him through me, without having to use words. I remembered the saying often attributed to St. Francis of Assisi: "Preach the gospel at all times; when necessary, use words." The human part of me yearned to share more with him about the God who loved him, regardless of the fact that he did not want to know. I knew our time together was limited, and I was not quick to forget the fact that he did not want to hear about Jesus!

As I was praying alone one afternoon, I felt the Holy Spirit leading me to "practice" telling James about Jesus. We all know when the Holy Spirit is prompting us, and it is most often because we know we could not have come up with the idea on our own. Sometimes, too, it is because we simply do not want to do what He is prompting us to do, and we find ourselves digging in our heels. The idea of "practicing" telling someone about Jesus was foreign to me, but I decided to obey. That night I went for a walk with a friend and asked her if I could "practice" sharing Jesus with her in preparation for my spending time with James, although I did not know when that would be. She agreed.

The miracle of all of this was that when I sensed the Holy Spirit's prompting the day before, James was no more actively dying at that moment than I was. However, first thing the next morning, I received a call from triage saying that he was experiencing a dramatic decline and needed my attention immediately. I arrived to find him in bed, confused, incontinent, with complete weakness in his legs and body, and his wife totally beside herself. I called my supervisor and arranged to have him transported to a private room at the Hospice Center. There, he and his family could be together without the stress of caring for him at home during these new and rapid changes.

When we got him settled in bed and resting peacefully, I was able to spend some time with him alone before I went to see other patients. I got down on my knees to the right of his bed, and I said to him, "James." He answered, "Yes," while his eyes remained closed. "You have been sharing with me for six months now about your gods, and I was wondering if you might let me tell you a little bit about mine." He responded, "Okay," with his eyes still closed. We had become friends by this time, speaking and listening to each other well, and thankfully I had earned the right to share my God and the gospel of Jesus Christ with him. He trusted me.

So I told him about the God who loved him beyond all measure, the God who knew him and whose love would go beyond time and knowledge, the Creator of the universe, the Father of us all. I knew James could understand and identify with the "person" the Father reflected. He began to relax. I then told him about the Christ, the Son sent by the Father, who by His life, death, and resurrection had opened the door to eternal life for us and who forgives all of our transgressions. This Christ knew and loved him better than he would ever know or love himself. James had come to the point of wanting to listen, wanting to hear and understand, and I assured him that he only had to reach out his hand and accept God's love to spend eternity with the true lover of his soul.

Christ's love was reflected through me. This is the work of the Holy Spirit; we know it is never ourselves but He in us, drawing His children to His own heart. The love and patience God had given me captivated James, and he wanted to know where it came from. As I was kneeling by the side of his bed, I whispered into his ear, holding his hand; James's expression was now so peaceful, with no guard, no defense. His eyes remained closed the whole time. I knew for sure that God was present to him in ways I could not see, and I trusted His compassionate heart to lead James home.

After I shared with him all about God's redeeming love, his eyes remained closed for a short time. I wondered if he had comprehended anything I had said. When finally he opened his eyes, he smiled and gently said to me, "Are you finished now?"

"Yes," I said, "I am finished now."

He squeezed my hand gently and closed his eyes, saying, "I love you too." He died a few hours later peacefully in his sleep. I knew for sure that God had his heart and was holding him in the palm of His hand.

God was with James all his life, but the answers James had been looking for had eluded him until just before his death. I believe he was carried into heaven and placed in the arms of his Savior, who presented Himself to James in the way he could accept Him best.

Jessica

"Last night, this beautiful man came into my room, dressed all in white"

Jackie Aquino

Jessica was seventy-two years old and had been my neighbor for many years. She had one son who lived out of town, and she did not see him often. Her sister-in-law, who lived nearby, was a very close friend and was at her bedside every day.

She knew I was a Hospice nurse, and over the years we had spoken many times about God and how I saw Him daily in the terminally ill and dying patients in my care. She believed in God but had spent many years going from church to church, seeking a peace she was unable to find. She knew that God loved and cared for her, but she wanted a more intimate relationship with Him than she had been able to have, and this made her very sad. Each time we spoke together about Him, she said she felt His presence a little bit more, and the times we shared meant a great deal to both of us.

Jessica had been diagnosed with breast cancer years ago, and now it had returned in her lungs with a vengeance, spreading to other parts of her body as well. She had been hospitalized recently, hopeful of either getting better or at least feeling better, but that was not meant to be. When she returned home, I spent many days visiting with her, and on one such occasion she said to me, "Jackie, I know now that I am not going to get any better, not this time." In the past, she had always been able to hold back the tears that were just below the surface, but today she could no longer do that. "I'm dying, Jackie," she said to me. "I need you to pray with me now."

And so we did. The prayers flowed from my heart as well as hers, and there is no doubt in my mind that Jesus Himself was ministering to her. It is an amazing experience when God places you in a circumstance like this, when you sense beyond any question that you are simply the vehicle through which God is comforting His children. This is what He is speaking about when He tells us to love one another as He has loved us.

As I mentioned earlier, for years Jessica had been visiting churches in an effort to find one she was comfortable with, and one day she said to me, "If I had the time now, I would become a Catholic, but it's too late—or is it? The one place I visited where I felt most at home was your Holy Family Catholic Church. Do you think your priest would come to visit me?"

Our pastor was only a phone call away, and Jessica's request was answered immediately. During the priest's visit, Jessica was in that place of "quiet reverie" that I have seen so often. It can last two to three days, after which the person will communicate again, sometimes in a completely new way. She was aware of everything going on about her but not responsive, so the priest prayed over her, asking

God to bless her in a special way and to take her home with Him gently, when the time was right. Jessica had searched for a place she could find God's peace, and now she seemed to have found it.

Our Lord loves us to look for Him and to search for Him, through all the seasons of our lives. He tells us to "ask and you will receive; seek and you will find; knock and the door will be opened to you" (Luke 11:9). It is an awesome privilege as a Hospice nurse to see up close what happens between our heavenly Father and one of His children as He is drawing them to Himself. It is mercy and love personified and reflected in ways we can barely grasp. At times, it simply takes our breath away.

By now all my visits with Jessica took place at the Hospice Center. She could no longer remain at home alone, as she was getting weaker each day. On one of my last visits with her, she said to me, "I'm going to tell you something that I can't tell anyone else, because I know you'll understand and won't think I'm crazy." She pointed to a specific area in her room. "Last night, this beautiful man came into my room, right there. He was dressed all in white and was very, very tall. He had beautiful, piercing eyes, but he did not speak to me. I seemed to be completely surrounded by love, which radiated directly from his eyes. I'm not sure if he was an angel or if he was Jesus Himself, but today I feel a whole new peace and I am not afraid at all."

An early morning call from her son gave her permission to "go" whenever she felt it was time and brought a wonderful smile to her face. Her sister-in-law and I were with her at three that afternoon when she entered heaven. Hers was a beautiful and gentle death. Jessica had come full circle in her longing to be with the God she loved so much and to receive His peace.

Can you hear Jesus's words now: "Peace I leave with you; my peace I give to you. Not as the world gives do I give it to you. Do not let your hearts be troubled or afraid" (John 14:27)?

Krista

"She loved him as deeply as Mary loved Jesus"

Trudy Harris

She was only fifty-eight years old, but she was dying of lung cancer. She was a gentle and wonderful woman and an extremely loving mother to a son and a daughter. She was divorced and had lived alone for many years.

I had the feeling when we first met that Krista kept many things close to her heart, seldom confiding in others. Krista depended on God the way some people depend on friends in their daily lives. She said she spoke to Him often about her worries and concerns about herself and her children's future. She could talk with Him about anything at all, knowing her concerns were safe with Him and that He would give her the answers to the questions she poured out to Him. The complete trust Krista placed in God must have touched His heart deeply. He loves us to run to Him like little children, and when He said, "Unless you turn and become like children, you will not enter the kingdom of heaven" (Matt. 18:3), this is what He was talking about. Krista did just that.

Living alone for many years is one thing; dying alone is something entirely different. Krista needed help now, and although her neighbors and church community knew of her illness, they hesitated to reach out to her for fear of overstepping their place in her life. Now more than ever she needed her family around her, and she needed her Lord to direct the rest of her life and theirs.

Her daughter, who lived close by, was married with several children and worked full-time. She loved her mother dearly but was not able to be available to her as much as she would have liked. But she did her best on weekends and in the evenings.

Krista's son, David, was a freelance artist living in California. Even though Krista loved her son with all her heart, she had not seen him in the last few years, which troubled her. When he was speaking to her on the phone one day, he realized just how sick she really was and flew home immediately. The "mother part" of Krista knew the moment she saw David that something was seriously wrong with him. He was thin and pale, frequently fatigued, and often very short of breath. He had a cough that he could not control, and although he was only in his early thirties, he looked much older.

It saddened Krista's heart to see her son so sick, and it pained David even more deeply that his mother had to see him this way. They had been very close as he was growing up, and the love between them was deep and strong. He had moved to California at a young age as a way of trying to find himself, and got caught up in a world he knew little about. In just a few years, he was very, very sick and did not want his mother to know, did not want her to worry or suffer because of him. When I first met him, I knew right away that Krista and David would probably die within weeks of each other. Although HIV and AIDS were somewhat new on the horizon in the early eighties, his illness was more than evident. We were hearing a great deal more about it in the medical field, and David surely was suffering its effects.

Here before us on a daily basis was a woman who was actively dying, lovingly cared for by her son, who was also dying. She loved him as deeply as Mary loved Jesus. She loved him with the unconditional love that Jesus speaks about and shows us often in the Gospels. To read about this love is one thing; to see it in action, on both their parts, was something else entirely.

David loved Krista with all of his heart and she him, and at this stage in their lives, that was all that mattered. Krista and her son spoke often and openly about Jesus and heaven. You could tell that this was not new for David. He had been searching for meaning and purpose and God for a long time. He would nod his head in recognition and with deep respect; acknowledging all she had to say to him. She in turn listened closely to all God had imparted in David's heart during his years of searching. It brought her unspeakable peace to hear that he knew the Lord and trusted in His compassionate love.

There is nothing quite so powerful as a mother's prayers for her children. Think of just how often Jesus told us to ask Him about the things we need and He would answer us. The answer to Krista's prayers was sitting with her now and preparing her for the eternal reward that Jesus had promised to both of them. Our God is such an awesome God. He not only answered Krista's heartfelt prayer but also allowed her to see her prayer come to fruition in this most unique way. She watched her son serve her needs and care for her with the very love Jesus had taught him. He was doing now for his mother what Jesus had done all His life.

David was with her for only about four weeks. Krista died one evening with him holding her, safe and unafraid.

He knew that he would be with her in heaven. He told me that he spoke to Krista often, picturing her with Jesus and knowing he would be with her there himself very soon.

David flew back home following his mother's funeral service. He died several weeks later in his home in California, surrounded by friends who loved him as well. I have no doubt in my mind that he was in full communion with Jesus, who had watched over him his entire life.

It is impossible to fathom the enormity of God's love for all of His children. He loves us all the time and remains with us, without distinction, until we are safely home with Him. He does not wait until we are perfect. If He did, He would be waiting forever for all of us, since perfection belongs to God alone. Remember Jesus telling of the shepherd who has many sheep but is unable to find one that is missing from the fold. He leaves all the other sheep and goes out to find the one that is still wandering alone. We are all that one sheep at different times in our lives, and Jesus simply stays with us until we find our way back to Him. We can never fully understand what the word *love* means from God's perspective. But we will one day, when we are with Him.

Sarah

"He will baptize you in the Holy Spirit"

Bonnie Tingley

Sarah was seventy-eight years old and dying of metastatic breast cancer. When I met her for the first time, she seemed resigned, knowing her time on earth was coming to an end. Sarah was not overly sad as she spoke about her remaining time. To the contrary, she felt she had lived a full and fulfilling life and was ready for the journey home. Jesus, she said, was her Lord and Savior, and for her, heaven was a reality. Sarah knew she was going to be with her Lord in heaven, and she happily looked forward to seeing Him there soon.

Sarah's family was supportive and tried to do everything they could to help her through the ups and downs of good and bad days and her approaching death. She was a mother, grandmother, and great-grandmother, and her desire was to die with dignity, surrounded by her large family, peaceful and unafraid. Slowly, I managed to meet everyone in her family as they took turns caring for her.

Brothers from Sarah's church met with her on a regular schedule, providing prayer, spiritual counseling, and Bible readings. She physically remained comfortable, but spiritually, for some reason, she was not at peace. During my conversation with her on one particular afternoon, she confided in me that although she had always believed in Jesus Christ as her Lord and Savior, she had never been baptized in church.

The brothers from her church talked to her about the necessity of being baptized and offered to baptize her by immersion in her bathtub, since she could not go outdoors to the church. The teachings of their church were such that if you were not baptized by full immersion, you would not go to heaven. Sarah was feeling anxious about all of the ramifications of what they were saying to her. She wanted so badly to be baptized, but she knew too just how weak and frail she was and that the time left to her was very short. Her daughter, who was intimately involved in her day-to-day care, was adamant that baptism by immersion was just not physically possible for Sarah, and I could not have agreed with her more.

Sarah and her daughter asked if I would call her church and speak with them about alternatives. The family was sure that if I called and explained the circumstances of her dying to the elders, they would relent. I made the call and spoke with the head elder, who told me that indeed it was the rule of his church, and nothing less than full immersion would meet the obligations for her baptism. "This church does not recognize sprinkle baptism," he said. The head elder then asked me, "Does she have a pool in her backyard?" Surely he was not suggesting what I thought he was! Since getting Sarah into the tub was impossible, he felt a pool was the next best option. The elder said that he thought it would work if the process was done quickly. I explained to him that Sarah was very ill, was close to death, and could not be put into a pool. It was February in northern Florida, and we were experiencing a cold snap, so the water temperature was much too cold for her body to handle—and moving her in that way was not possible either.

Our conversation ended with both of us feeling defeated, as we seemed to be at an impasse. I was especially down because Sarah's family was counting on me to see to Sarah's wishes to be baptized into the family of Jesus Christ.

Sarah and her daughter discussed all the options with me. The family asked for my thoughts on baptism, its meaning and its purpose. I replied that in my denomination baptism into Christ did not depend on the amount of water used. Rather baptism centers on Christ's desire to make all of His children part of His own family. It seemed to me that if Jesus Himself were present right now at Sarah's bedside, His compassionate heart would make this as simple as possible for His child. The family agreed after much discussion that the only option available was for me to contact the Hospice chaplain and ask him to visit with Sarah. The family would decide with her what they wanted to do after that visit.

The Hospice chaplain was a godly man named George, and he arrived in the afternoon to visit with Sarah and her family. After a long and meaningful discussion with them, Sarah made a decision: she would receive a "sprinkle baptism." Reverend George performed this important and holy service in her bedroom, with all the family gathered around her. It seemed as if this experience was what she had been waiting for all her life, and it brought her full circle into the family of her Lord and Savior, Jesus Christ. Sarah died peacefully a few days later, assured that she was baptized into His family and accepted in His eyes. As I drove home that night, the words of John the Baptist rang in my mind: "I have baptized you with water; he will baptize you with the holy Spirit" (Mark 1:8).

During my years in Hospice nursing, I often asked myself, "What would Jesus do in this instance?" As believers, we must be careful not to think we have all the answers, that we understand Jesus completely and how He loves and thinks. Scripture tells us in many ways that His mind and His ways are far above our ways, and however loving and compassionate we might be, we cannot fully comprehend the compassionate heart of Christ.

Jim

"I am sending someone who will know just what to say"

Bonnie Tingley

Jim was a fifty-six-year-old man dying of colon cancer. He was gentle and soft-spoken, a man of few words. He seemed to want to make the most of the few words he wanted to speak, and so he chose them wisely. Peg was his wife, and together they had three wonderful children: one in high school, one in junior high, and one in grade school. Both Jim and Peg worked in a dairy just a stone's throw away from their own backyard. As Jim's involvement with the dairy became more and more restricted, Peg would run in and out of the house all day long to check on him while at the same time continuing to work. The dairy owners were kind to them and allowed Peg the freedom she needed to keep working while caring for Jim. Both Jim and Peg spoke many times about how thankful they were to God for the understanding and support of their employers.

They spoke with me about wanting to make the most of whatever time God was going to give them. Jim's main worry was his family and their ability to make it on their own when he was no longer with them. I visited them over a period of several months as Jim began to experience a slow but steady decline.

Jim shared with me, as did Peg, that their church was literally holding them together both spiritually and physically. Their gifts of prayer, home visits, and meals met many of their day-to-day needs. Faith in God was uppermost in their minds and hearts. The brothers and sisters in the church reflected Christ's love and generosity, and it meant a great deal to both of them. The Scriptures come alive in these instances, and you can almost hear St. Paul speaking about caring for the widowed and the orphans.

I made a nursing visit early in the week, knowing full well I would need to check on them again as the week progressed. Jim seemed much weaker with each visit. His appetite was lessening and he was sleeping more and more every day. These are common signs that let us know when the body is beginning to shut down and getting ready to transition into a new life, which we call eternity. People who have a very deep and abiding faith in God long to see Him at this point and want to go on to the heaven they know has been prepared for them since the beginning of time. They are seldom afraid, and Jim was getting closer to this phase with each passing day.

I arrived home to do some paperwork in the afternoon and thought about calling Peg to see how Jim was doing. As I entered my house, the phone began to ring. Peg was calling to say that although Jim's breathing was extremely shallow and he was exhibiting all the signs and symptoms of impending death, he seemed unable for some reason to be at peace and to let go. Jim's pastor was present and had been praying with him all afternoon. Even so, nothing seemed to be helping, and Peg asked if I would come right away to be with them.

I jumped into my car and sped the distance to their home in record time. The drive was a good thirty minutes, and I felt sure by the time I arrived that Jim would have died. But that was not what God had in mind. Pulling up to the house, I was surprised to see a number of cars there. I entered the front door and was taken to a small bedroom full of people quietly standing around. It was actually hard to get through all the family and church friends at Jim's bedside. Sitting at the head of the bed, holding Jim's hand in hers, was his lovely wife, Peg. All three children were on the bed with their dad.

I quietly prayed for the words to accomplish what the Lord wanted me to do at this time to help both Jim and his family. Words came to me directly from the Holy Spirit, I know. I whispered softly to Jim that Peg had his hand in hers, and that Jesus was holding the other one. I reminded him that Jesus loved him and his family dearly, and He would take care of them and provide for all of them. I told him that even though he loved them very much, Jesus loved them even more. Peg and the children would be well cared for by this room full of good people. Now it was time for him to let go and go on to God. I assured him that the time was right. I told him that when he felt comfortable and ready, that he could simply let go of Peg's hand and follow Jesus, who was holding his other hand. He became immediately calm and died in an instant, very peacefully. Husbands often wait until "someone in charge" comes to be with their loved ones. It is as if, until the very end, they want to be sure their family has the loving support and care they need.

When it was time for me to leave, a young man approached me and introduced himself as Jim's pastor. He told me he had been praying hard for quite some time about what to say to Jim and his family. The pastor was a close friend of Jim's and found it hard to find the right words to say. Then, in his prayer time, the Lord spoke to him softly but clearly, saying, "I am sending someone who will know just what to say." The pastor felt that what he had just seen happen was God's promise fulfilled in that very room.

I am reminded of the Scripture story that tells of Jesus approaching Jerusalem and sending two disciples ahead into the city to retrieve a colt. Jesus tells His disciples that if the colt's owner has a question, to simply tell him, "The Master needs it," and he will somehow have been prepared by the Holy Spirit to already know of this.

When God calls us to a certain work, we know it. He prepares the ground He asks us to walk on ahead of time. He gives us everything we will need to minister to His children and to bring them home safely to Him. And in some way that we will only understand later on, He ministers to us at the same time.

I know of no other experience that is filled with greater peace and joy than to walk someone into heaven. It is a rare and sacred moment and one in which you feel you can reach up and touch the face of God. We are simply vessels through which He makes Himself known to His children. Very humbling indeed.

Douglas

"His little hands reached up and tried to open the lid of the casket"

Nikki Fox-Nash

It has been nineteen years since my brother Douglas died. For many years, I have tried to write about what it was like to be a sister losing her "little brother," and an aunt watching her small nephews experience the death of their dad. At the time, Douglas was thirty-five, going through a divorce, and the father of three young boys. Kevin, the oldest, was ten, and the twins Christopher and Derrick were eight.

His illness began as the flu. Our dad called the doctor when Douglas could not get his fever to go down after a few weeks of self-medicating. The doctor gave Douglas antibiotics, but when he did not respond after four weeks, the doctor admitted him to the hospital, where they discovered he had lymphoma. This disease strikes all ages, men and women alike, and at times can be treated successfully. At other times, the disease can be swift and unrelenting. The prayers of our families, friends, and church groups were nonstop. We literally stormed heaven with petitions for a cure for Douglas. The situation was all in God's hands, and His thoughts about healing were different from ours.

God blessed me with many wonderful people in my life during this time: my dad; my husband, Denis; my brother David; and close friends from St. Peter's. Two of my dearest church friends, Pat and David O'Steen, were a godsend. David and Douglas became fast friends, which is often the way God lets things happen for His own purposes, and often not understood by us at the time. David could identify with Douglas; he himself had gone through a lengthy battle with cancer. He was also a great support to my dad and to Kevin. He spent his lunch hours visiting Douglas, and together they shared their love for Christ and their families.

That summer Dad became the main caregiver for both Douglas and Kevin, while the twins stayed with their mother. During those seven months, from diagnosis until his death, many things happened all at the same time. Douglas was in the middle of a divorce, all the while going in and out of the hospital. The children attended Vacation Bible School, then started a new school year, then celebrated Thanksgiving and Christmas while snow covered Jacksonville, Florida, for three whole days. Douglas died on January 3, followed by his viewing and funeral and then the time to say a final good-bye. God's grace alone carried us through this period of time that seemed to vanish before our eyes.

If I had known that would be the last Thanksgiving we would have with Douglas, I would not have gone away for the holiday or at least not stayed away so long. I believed there would be other Thanksgivings; the doctor had said that Douglas was in remission and there was no sign of cancer anywhere. My brother was supposed to be getting better; he was even looking and feeling much better. But that was not to be.

Douglas became very sick a few days after Thanksgiving and went back into the hospital. He was able to come home for Christmas and spend a little time with his boys, but not for long. A few days before the New Year he called me at work and said, "Nikki, Dad is taking me back to the hospital. I don't want to go. If I go, I know I won't ever leave there again." His words pierced my heart so deeply that I thought it would break.

By the time I got to the hospital with Douglas's oldest son, Kevin, my brother was on a respirator and attached to every kind of pump, IV, and tubing I could imagine. We were praying so hard for a miracle. Douglas, after all, was a young man with three wonderful sons whom he loved so much. Surely God did not plan to take him to heaven at thirty-five. We always pray that God's will be done, but in times like these, you just beg Him to see it your way.

Douglas went into a coma on New Year's Eve, and the next day the doctor told us that Douglas's body was shutting down and there was nothing more he could do. It was a heartbreaking moment for everyone: the little boys who would no longer have a father, the sister and brother who would no longer have their little brother to tease anymore, and the dad whose young, energetic son would go to heaven before him. Little Christopher's plea, "I just want to hold Daddy," was not to be. Christopher had a cold, and in those days, children were not allowed near a very sick person. In today's world of Hospice care, we are much more enlightened. I wonder if anyone explained to Christopher that you do not need to be physically present with someone as they die. Everyone they have ever loved or who has ever loved them is "present" to the dying person as they die. The physical presence is not as important as the love they share, which has no boundaries and makes itself known in ways understood only by God. But for an eight-year-old, no reason or explanation could possibly comfort his heart. He just wanted "to hold Daddy, one more time."

My dad's hand shook so hard when he signed the form to have the respirator turned off. I could not even begin to imagine the courage and love it took to be able to do this. He placed Douglas's hand in his and began to cry then sob deeply as he crumpled to his knees at the side of Douglas's bed. He stayed that way for a long time, and nobody moved. Douglas died thirty minutes later. It was the first time I had ever seen my dad cry. God the Father, giving up His Son, Jesus, must have felt something like this. He knew it was necessary to save a hurting world, but the pain to God the Father's own heart had to be somehow like my dad's pain in letting Douglas go. When God the Father came to this earth through His Son, He fully shared the humanity we all know so well. Jesus had a divine and a human nature. Every emotion we will ever experience, Jesus understands perfectly.

The morning of the funeral service was a blur. I remember watching the children as they sat by Douglas's casket in the front pew. When the service began, they closed the casket for the last time. For a moment I thought of life for my brother David and me without Douglas, and my dad without his son. Then my mind went immediately to Douglas's children and what life without him would mean to them for years to come.

When the service was over and it was time for the family to proceed to the receiving room, I noticed little Christopher turn away from the procession and walk back to the casket. I stepped out of line to watch him as he stood staring at it. His little hands reached up and tried to open the lid, and I realized he wanted to see his daddy one more time.

We beckoned to the funeral director, who came right over and helped Christopher lift the lid on his dad's casket. His twin brother, Derrick, and ten-year-old brother,

Kevin, hurried to the casket as well. Who will ever know what thoughts are in the minds of children so young when they see their dad lying in a large shiny box and someone they do not know closes the lid on him. The sadness and finality of it all must be beyond their heart's comprehension, and only God can bring understanding to them later in their lives.

Quietly within my heart, I prayed to the Holy Spirit for guidance for me and comfort for the children, which by now included all the cousins, David, Rebecca, and Ben. I asked the children if they would like to make a bouquet of flowers for Douglas. It seemed like the right thing to do, and they were delighted to be asked.

I stepped back to watch them carefully pick the flowers from the sprays and arrangements around the church. Then they gently laid them on and around Douglas's body, each child taking his or her turn and carefully placing a flower where they wanted it to be. When each child was satisfied with what they had done, they walked away from the casket and stood by me. It was their very own good-bye.

One month after the funeral, I had a dream. In my dream, I was standing in an open field surrounded by beautiful, billowy white clouds. Suddenly I noticed someone walking toward me and smiling. It was Douglas. "You're dead," I said softly. He smiled at me and said, "Yes. I have a message for you to give to my sons; tell them I am with Jesus now and that I love them very much." For just a moment, the veil was lifted between heaven and earth, and God the Father allowed this gift to be given to Kevin, Derrick, and Christopher. He understood a father's love all too well and sent this once-in-a-lifetime gift so they could remember it forever.

Lois

"She never wavered in her commitment to what is of God"

Dottie Dorion

First impressions are often lasting impressions, and so it was with Lois. At a study group looking into problem issues related to our city, I sat across the conference table from a regal lady in her mid-sixties with fluffy white hair and a legal pad and pen at hand. When the discussion began, it was obvious that this was going to be another one of those conversations in the Deep South of the 1970s that were taken over by "the good ol' boys."

This was how our study group began, but not for long. This feisty lady just kept presenting facts (she had done her homework), and she silenced all of us with her knowledge, retorts, and persistence in making her case. Even at a first meeting, I knew she would not take no for an answer. She would persevere if she knew the cause was right and good. She was a lawyer, was married to a classmate lawyer and judge, had raised five children, and had become one of the first female attorneys in the state of Florida. I knew I had indeed found a very rare "bird" and an extraordinary friend.

In the late seventies, Hospice was just beginning to emerge nationally. In our city, a group of interested people gathered at a church to hear about the "Hospice concept of care," which was to keep dying patients in their home, with a support team of volunteers, both lay and professional. Our Hospice adventures were the beginning of long and lasting friendships between Lois and me and several others sharing the same goal, which we called the "Group of Six." As we worked together from meager beginnings with a chair and desk under the stairs for our office and one patient in her own home, the concept began to develop and grow. Lois, in her Hospice and other community projects, reflected that she lived the words of Jesus, "You shall love the Lord, your God, with all your heart, with all your being, with all your strength, and with all your mind, and your neighbor as yourself" (Luke 10:27).

She found unfairness in a restrictive Hospice law that required Hospices to own a hospital bed in one location, far from the patient's own family and doctor. That law put all grassroots programs in violation, and the heart of Hospice, which was home care, would become hospital based if the law had its way. Lois would never compromise her strong belief that she was to use her God-given gifts and talents to do what was just and fair for everyone. So she, together with two others, became lobbyists at the state capitol with the goal of changing the Hospice law. If she had her way, patients could remain at home, keeping their own doctor, and would not have to go to a hospital far from home rather than one near them if that need should arise.

Lois had a mind like a fine steel trap, and her brilliant legal brain could decipher the mumbo jumbo of not only the law but politics as well. Eventually, corrections to the law were made without a dissenting vote, in large part due to Lois and her unfailing faith that God's will would be accomplished and that the patient always came first, no matter what.

My friendship with Lois continued as our Group of Six volunteered our time, energy, and resources to move the "Hospice Concept of Caring" forward well into the eighties and mid-nineties. This friendship continued for decades, and our discussions were often heated and humorous but never dull. I came to believe that the greater the challenge, the stronger Lois's faith became. No matter how difficult the road, Lois never wavered in her commitment to what is of God. Before every meal we shared, we said grace, which was often a long and intimate way of asking for God's blessings on our work and our families, for help with the needs at hand, and for peace in our world. It was a wonderfully loving group that had God as its leader from the start.

As the years passed, we entered the new millennium with our Group of Six becoming a Group of Five then a Group of Four. About this time, Lois began to have many new medical problems, becoming frailer with each hospital admission and discharge. We continued to meet regularly at her lovely home as we always had, but her decline was more apparent with each visit. Lunch went from her elaborate, home-cooked feasts that she had always delighted in preparing to a lighter fare of finger sandwiches or takeout. She often smiled and said to us, "I'm not feeling too well today. I think I need a new body." Times were different now, and she relied on God and those He put around her to make this time as good as it could possibly be for her.

Some days, with the help of her children, Lois would get out of bed to lunch with us. We knew when she did not get her hair done on Friday or attend church on Sunday that she was really feeling badly. Her supportive family, most of them nearby, checked on her each day, and one daughter in London called frequently. Her pills were laid out for her with loving care, and she could still enjoy looking out at the beautiful St. Johns River from every room in her home.

As Lois declined, she developed increased pain, weakness, and loss of appetite. Her disease had spread to the abdominal area, and she reluctantly agreed to leave her beautiful home to be admitted into the Hospice Center for Caring that she had made possible through her hard, God-directed work so many years earlier. She was now reaping what she herself had sown—dying peacefully with her friends and family around her and the doctor of her own choosing. Only now, there was not just one patient being well cared for but over a thousand patients receiving care every day in the way they wished to receive it. Everything comes full circle. You receive, in one way or another, by God's own design, all that you have given to others. God cannot be outdone in generosity, ever.

Lois had a beautiful, large, sunny room, and during her first few weeks there, family and friends came and went all day long. Everyone who visited could not help but notice the shelves of trophies, awards, plaques—every example of honors paying tribute to her lifetime of service to those in need—that her family had placed around the room. The steady stream of visitors came from all walks of life, because Lois had reached out to people regardless of race, creed, or color. She touched everyone she met and changed lives for the better in every area of the community she served. "The old gang" still came by, but now we just had a Coke and chocolates, which were graciously offered by the "lady in charge." It was interesting that when family members were present, she often slept but when the old gang appeared, she became her "old self" and continued her jokes, puns, arguments, and reminiscing.

As Lois became weaker and less responsive, she discussed with me concerns that had to be resolved before she could "go on" in peace. She had a beloved grandchild who had gotten into trouble at college. He was scheduled to be home soon, but as a Hospice nurse, I thought perhaps not soon enough. She needed to see this grandchild one last time, but time was running out. It was in God's hands now.

Many of God's gifts began to unfold as Lois rested securely in His arms. One morning a harpist came by and played at her bedside. Lois's son, Bill, was holding her hand on one side of the bed while I held her hand on the other side. Many family members were scattered around the room. We were instructed to be quiet while the harpist played the hymns and classical music Lois loved so much. Her son had tears running down his cheeks, as we all did, while trying not to move or wipe our noses. We were perfectly still and were lifted by the very real presence of the Holy Spirit in her room. Lois, who had been asleep, responded when Bill asked her how she liked it. She said in a weak little voice, "It was just beautiful."

We were definitely running out of time, and Lois was sleeping more and talking less. Her daughter from London was to arrive shortly, but our prayer that Lois would stay until her grandchild came home was growing only remotely possible.

When Lois celebrated her ninetieth birthday, each family member contributed a special square to a quilt, which the family presented to her. This included children, grandchildren, and a great-granddaughter. The quilt hung high on the wall of her living room for all visitors to see. It had wonderful messages made from college banners, personal clothing, photos, stories, trips, and on and on. Her daughter from Boston, who had been present for several weeks, decided that Mom had to have her family quilt surrounding her. She climbed up the ladder, retrieved the quilt, and brought it to the Hospice center. On what was to be her final day, as Lois was sleeping peacefully, her grandson arrived and went to his grandmother's bedside, letting her know he was there. She opened her eyes and squeezed his hand as he laid his face next to hers. God had answered her prayers one more time, letting her know that this much-loved grandson was safe in His hands. As all the family gathered at the bedside, Lois lay wrapped in her family quilt of many colors and went quietly to her heavenly reward, knowing that she had truly completed the work God had given her to do. God's will be done on earth as it is in heaven is indeed a reality.

Ronald

"We are often visited by angels unaware"

Lois-Anne Isabelle

Sometimes in life we have an experience that scratches an old and beloved memory. And so it was with Ronald and me.

My family had lived a very simple life growing up; my father was a baker who worked long, late-night hours to provide for my sister and me as best he could. I am the eldest of two girls, and I remember hearing my dad often say, "I just love my girls."

When we were very little, my sister and I would go to a small local store like Woolworth's, Kresgee's, or Fishman's at Christmastime to buy a pair of pajamas, a belt, and peanut brittle to put under the tree for Dad. We were always happy that Dad, who was so good to us all the time, had some presents too. What we did not know until after his death was that he would put some of the gifts in the hallway cedar chest, so they could be taken out the next year, "brand new and shiny," he would say. "Not even out of the package yet." We were much too young to notice that they were often the same presents given the year before or to understand his desire for us to know how pleased he was with us for our generosity to him.

My sister and I never caught on, and the father who loved us so much and who worked so hard to give his family everything he could died at fifty-six years young of lung cancer.

Many years later, I met a man named Ronald who was living and dying on the streets of Jacksonville, Florida. He was admitted into the emergency room of the hospital where I worked as a supervisor on the weekends. He had lived on the street most of his life and had not had a pillow to lay his head on or a place to call home in decades—so long ago he could barely remember. "I have been a railroad man all of my life," he said. "I have been mending tracks, shoveling stones between the ties, and generally fixing anything that needed fixing, odd jobs, you know, just about anything." There were no complaints, no feeling sorry for himself, just Ronald stating the facts as they were.

One of Ronald's odd jobs was helping at a local thrift store. While he was working there, the persistent cough he had been dealing with had worsened. His energy was all but gone, and he found himself short of breath most of the time. His co-workers called 911 late one Friday afternoon when Ronald could not stop coughing and lost his breath completely. His co-workers thought they saw blood when he coughed, and he was taken directly to the hospital.

That was the afternoon I met Ronald, during his admission into the emergency room. This fifty-nine-year-old congenial and kindly man was obviously very, very sick. I had a long history of evaluating terminally ill patients, as my full-time position during the week was as a Hospice nurse, and I knew what I was looking at.

It took only a few tests to confirm Ronald's cancer of the lung. "I've got it real bad, or so they tell me," he said to me as I entered the room. The doctor in the emergency room had removed more than a quart of fluid from his lung almost immediately and had given him oxygen, which allowed him to be more comfortable and breathe easier within a short period of time.

When the ER doctor broke the news to Ronald, he sat in his bed, listening quietly, not saying a word. He did not seem disturbed by the news as much as he was by the questions that had no answers. "Now what?" he said to me. "Where will I stay? Who will take care of me? I have no family, no insurance, and no social security number." Ronald became quiet and introspective, trying to solve the rest of his life's dilemma. He did not want to be a burden to anyone; he did not want to complain or put anyone out, but this new challenge was very real for him.

Who did this kindly fifty-nine-year-old man with lung cancer remind me of? It came to me in a flash. His quiet independence, his desire not to be a burden, and his gentle manner brought my father's memory back to me in such a beautiful and real way. I would do anything to make Ronald's brief time left on earth as good as it could possibly be. In fact, everyone in the ER was determined to help this gentle soul for the little time he had left.

With my long experience as a Hospice nurse, I recognized how seriously ill Ronald was. His need to feel safe and settled and comfortable was all-important to me. We arranged a room for Ronald at a long-term care facility directly across the street from the hospital. We set out on a quest to ensure that he had the comfort and support he needed to ease his final days: books, music, a small TV and DVD player, and of course many visits from our Hospice team made up of nurses, social workers, and volunteers. The nursing home staff also took to Ronald immediately, and cared for him with tender loving concern. We made sure that his sweet tooth was satisfied for as long as he could eat. He shared these treats with his roommates from the beginning, as he had done all his life. People who live on the streets know what it means to be hungry and cold. It is in circumstances such as this that you see clearly the compassionate heart of Jesus in action. You see His face in theirs.

I purchased two pairs of pajamas, a robe, and slippers for Ronald the day after settling him in at the long-term care facility. Doing so reminded me of the pajamas in the cedar chest saved from year to year by my father so long ago. It was as if my dad was standing right next to me, guiding me in my every thought and effort.

Ronald and my father were connected in some way that I did not fully understand. The experience with Ronald gave me a feeling of completeness, as if I was doing for my dad all over again. I think God allows us to experience Him in these "moments of light" repeatedly throughout our lives, and it is so good when we are open to recognizing Him.

On one of my last visits with Ronald, he gave me back one of the pairs of pajamas I had given to him. Brand new and shiny . . . not even out of the packaging yet. "Here, angel," he said to me. "Take these, I won't be needing them anymore now. Please give them to someone who does, and thank you for all that you have done to make me feel so special."

I really do believe that Jesus presents Himself to us in many disguises, and He simply wants to see how we will respond. In truth, what we do for others, we really do for Him. Jesus told us in the Scriptures that we are often visited by angels unaware. I had to ask myself, "Is this one of the times that Jesus was referring to?" It sure felt that way. Regardless of who Ronald was, my experience with him was wonderful and memorable, bringing my dad back to me in a most intimate and loving way.

Ronald died just a few weeks after he came into the emergency room. Everyone involved felt it was clear that God did not want Ronald to die alone on the street, which is why He sent him to us. In his dying, Ronald continued to think compassionately of others. No matter how little he had, he wanted to share it with those who had less. I will always be grateful to God for sending Ronald my way.

Ellen

"Something is holding her; you need to find out what it is"

Trudy Harris

Life had been hard for Ellen from the beginning. She had a child when she was only fifteen years old and had been on her own for all of the child's early years; she simply yearned for a normal life and someone to love her. So often, young people who do not feel connected for any number of reasons—death, separation, divorce—look hard for that safe place where they can find some semblance of order and peace. They long to be accepted and to belong to someone. A baby, though very loved, did not do for Ellen what she had hoped for, and she was forced to raise her son on her own, which was difficult.

By the time she was thirty, she had been married to a good man for a few years, but her oldest son was a rebellious fifteen-year-old and had gotten into drugs. She realized he was now at the age she had been when she gave birth to him, but he would not stay in school or observe any of the family rules. This caused disruption for the entire family, which now included three little ones. In desperation, she did the only thing she thought would help the rest of her family. She made the very hard decision to have him leave the home, since no amount of discipline or intervention redirected his drug use or his lifestyle.

For the next twenty years, she and her husband raised a happy, well-adjusted family of three children. Although she didn't hear from her eldest son again, he was never out of her heart or her prayers.

Now in her early fifties, Ellen was dying of end-stage pancreatic cancer, which had spread to many other parts of her body. Her husband and children loved her dearly, and she had done well by all of them. They had grown up to be fine men and women, and the thought of life without their mother was impossible for them to comprehend. Unable to remain at home because of her uncontrolled pain, she was admitted into the Hospice Center for care. She rested pain free and comfortable for the first time in quite a long time. Something, however, seemed to be keeping her from the peace that she and everyone else were hoping for. "Something is holding her," her insightful and caring surgeon said to me one day. "You need to find out what it is. She's lived much longer than we could have expected, and she is suffering on many levels."

Ellen's husband felt that for his wife to let go and die well, she would need final closure with her firstborn child. After many conversations within the extended family, an aunt admitted that she had remained somewhat connected to him over the years. She gave me his phone number, and I called him that day, explaining the circumstances of his mother's medical condition and her need to see him again. It was hard to imagine that this thirty-five-year-old, well-spoken young man was the son of a fifty-year-old dying mother who'd had to insist he leave the home so many years ago. He was wonderful to speak with and wanted to visit her immediately. He needed to see how quickly he could get the funds together for a flight from California to Florida.

Esprit de Corp, a group of young professionals in our community, had been creating awareness and fund-raising events for the benefit of our Hospice patients for many years. I called them immediately, sharing the plight of this mother and son and the need to get him to her as soon as possible. The wheels began to turn immediately, and a fund-raising event was set up for that very weekend. A wine tasting at a small well-known bistro was arranged, with all proceeds going to the flight costs of this important visitor.

Esprit de Corp was a group of strongly committed professionals who had chosen Hospice as their "cause." Their founders were young executives in corporations, law firms, financial houses, banking, marketing, and public relations, and they knew how to do their jobs very well. This group was so highly respected and well known that the mere mention of the name Esprit de Corp brought corporate heads and those in local government and medicine to their feet. They worked tirelessly for many years, raising the important dollars needed to care for terminally ill and dying people. The Hospice program they chose to support would never be where it is now, serving one thousand patients each day, without their compassion, dedication, and support. In everything they did, they reflected the mind and heart of Jesus Himself, and they followed His lead in caring about others.

Esprit de Corp raised the money immediately, and the son arrived by the following weekend to be with his dying mother. The smiles I saw spread across the faces of everyone in the family as the door opened is forever etched in my mind. They simply fell into each other's arms amid tears and hugs and kisses. Half brothers and sisters surrounded them as well. Rembrandt himself could not have painted a more exquisite picture of love and forgiveness, joy and heartbreak, than this reunion at the end of a mother's life.

The door was closed behind them, leaving only a mother and son inside. He told me later how sorry his mother was to have sent him away. She told him that she felt she had so few resources at the time and tried to no avail to change him. She felt she simply had no other choice. He shared with her the fact that he always hated not having a father of his own and felt badly when his friends had their dads involved in their lives. Much of the time, he was sad that he did not have someone who was old enough to guide and love him, a sadness he covered with anger. He remembered how hard her husband had tried to be a father to him and how he had responded in ways that only made things worse. They understood each other's pain and inability to give to the other. They forgave, and forgave, and forgave each other, and it allowed them to experience a peace that can come only from the heart of God.

He told her that by God's grace alone, a wonderful family, well grounded in their Christian faith, had taken him in, and he had felt loved and understood for the first time in his life. Belonging to this family had enabled him to finish high school and to eventually, with help, graduate from college. Ellen saw, in person, the answer to the prayers she had said for so many years, begging God to keep this son in His care. He brought pictures of his young family, and Ellen was grateful to see the grandchildren she would not ever get to know on earth but would see later in heaven. She died three days later, at peace with her son and family and longing to see the face of her God.

Joseph

"Can you see the angels and the beautiful gold lights shining from them?"

Helen K. Basile

I was a young nurse, just four years out of St. Clare's Hospital School of Nursing in New York City. Our training by the beautiful Franciscan nuns prepared us well, not only to serve the physical needs of our patients but also to be open to seeing the face of Jesus in them.

My five-year-old cousin Joseph was in the hospital and scheduled to have his tonsils out. While there, the doctors discovered a lump in the side of his neck. This little guy, so young and so pure, was diagnosed with sarcoma, and at that time there was little to no hope for remission or a cure. Medicine has come a long way in the last forty years, but in those days, a diagnosis like Joseph's was a death sentence.

During the next few months, every effort was made to keep him comfortable and unafraid and to support his young parents, who were devastated. Two months after the initial diagnosis, Joseph was back in the hospital, a very sick little boy, and his time with us was growing short. There were no Hospices at that time, and it was the norm to remain in the hospital to die.

It was Eastertime, and I had promised to stay with him on Holy Saturday night, from four until midnight. "Can you see the angels and the beautiful gold lights shining from them?" Joseph asked. "The music is so beautiful too," he said. "Can you hear them singing?" I remember telling him that I could, because he would get upset whenever I did not answer him right away or when I said I could not see them too. Although this was a new experience for me, I did not doubt him or his experience for a moment. At the time, I wondered why I did not doubt what he was telling me.

He told me his dad was going to buy a new blue suit for him, and that he was going to wear it when he went to see Jesus. His dad called to check on him at about 10:00 p.m., and I told him Joseph was resting well and seemed peaceful. I shared with him all the things Joseph had told me about the angels and the beautiful music. His dad took it all in quietly, not saying a word but somehow knowing that Joseph was going to leave them. I finished my four-to-twelve shift and headed home, telling Joseph I would see him again the next day.

His parents had arranged for a private-duty nurse from twelve until eight in the morning, as in those days parents were not encouraged to stay overnight with a family member. Nursing staff at that time was not nearly as open to discussing the impending death of a child as they are today. If Hospice and end-of-life care was as understood and prevalent then as it is now, the nurses would have been talking to Joseph and his family about the immediacy of his going to heaven, and they in turn would have been better prepared. That was simply not done at the time, which made it more difficult for everyone. Death was shrouded in mystery.

I heard the phone ring in the hallway at home at around 7:00 a.m. and my mother crying. "Yes," she said. "I will go and tell her now." She came into my room and told me that the angels had come for Joseph at about 6:00 and had taken him into heaven with them. His dad was going to the store when they opened to buy a blue suit for Joseph, just as he had told me.

Although this experience happened forty-seven years ago, it is as fresh in my mind now as if it happened yesterday. When I read *Glimpses of Heaven*, the memory surfaced again so clearly in my mind, and the remembering of it made me smile.

When Jesus said to let the little children to come to Him for the kingdom of heaven belonged to them, I think this is what He was speaking about. The simplicity and purity of their lives is what Jesus was telling us to follow in order to be like Him. The confidence and trust Joseph reflected as he was dying is what Jesus wants us to experience throughout our lives. In that way, we will be at peace when it is our time to go home to Him.

Be open, always, to the youngest and the oldest around you. Jesus will make Himself known to you in some of the tenderest and most delicate ways you can ever imagine. The kingdom of God is all around us. You just have to reach out and touch it to follow in His footsteps.

Charlie

"He could not share the gospel boldly until he received the fullness of the Holy Spirit"

Gene H. Lewis

Charlie was a very bright physician who graduated from medical school second in his class and became a urologist six years later. He was in medical school during WWII and enlisted in the navy. As such, the government paid for his schooling, which was a huge help, as his family could not do so. He served thirty years all over the world, including Panama, Guam, Pensacola, San Diego, Jacksonville, Long Island, New York, Washington DC, and aboard the *Orion* submarine tender. When he left the navy, he became chief of urology at Shands Hospital in Jacksonville, Florida. He taught young residents there as a University of Florida instructor, just as he had done for eight years at the naval hospital in New York City. Some of the best urologists were trained under Dr. Charlie Lewis, and he took great pride in each of them.

Charlie was, first and foremost, a man of honor. He grew up during the Depression in a family that grew most of their own food. His father traveled a good bit of the time, and his mother and siblings did most of the farm work. His mother was a fine Christian woman, and her children were raised under her direction, attending church and learning all that she knew about the teachings of Jesus.

Charlie loved to sing and did so in college and in the Duke University Chapel Choir. He learned at an early age that we can praise God in many ways, one being through medicine and another through music and song. He did just that with gusto. We met at Duke when we were both in school there and were friends attending many of the same parties. The years passed quickly, and as the time grew closer to graduation, after our third year of a great friendship, we found we were in love and married the following November.

The night we were married, Charlie surprised me by suggesting that we pray together before going to bed. Although that was a big surprise to a new bride, I quickly learned what a great gift it would be to us over the years in every aspect of our lives. We welcomed four sons in succession. During their growing-up years, we traveled extensively, attending many churches of different denominations and leaving ourselves open to all Jesus had to say to us through their teachings. We learned a great deal, both from the denominations themselves and through the people of different traditions and beliefs that we came to know.

When we moved to Jacksonville, Charlie attended a weekend retreat known as Cursillo, which is an experience offered by many different Christian denominations through which a person meets the Lord in a whole new way. Charlie was never the same again.

By nature, Charlie was an introvert, and in the past he found sharing the Lord with others very difficult. He loved Him deeply, trusted Him implicitly, but like the apostles, he could not share the gospel boldly just yet—that is, until he received the fullness of the Holy Spirit.

After his Cursillo weekend, everything changed, and Charlie could go anywhere, speak to anyone, just as long as it was about the Father's love and all that He had done for us. He became involved serving prisoners at the state prison in Raiford, Florida. He attended a weekend retreat for the men there and then volunteered to help prisoners who were being released from prison to find a place to live, obtain a job, and hopefully better their lives. During that time and for many years after, Charlie brought many men to Christ, and I have letters from those men, written after Charlie's death, telling me how much he meant to them. He drove to the prison every Thursday to spend the day helping them. He sent Christmas cards to over one hundred men each year and sent many birthday cards as well. He prayed every morning for hundreds by name.

After he retired completely, he was scheduled to have back surgery, and during that time, the doctors discovered through blood tests that Charlie had chronic lymphatic leukemia. He faced this information the way he faced everything in life, with perfect trust that God would be with him through it all. And He was. The doctors followed Charlie carefully for several years until they reached the decision that he should begin chemo. As a man who had missed at the most two days of work all his life, he handled the decision very well and with great hope. Through many tough days, he remained fiercely independent and trusting in his Savior and Lord, and it was not until the last six months of his life that he reached for outside help.

God gave him the great gift of no pain, anywhere, ever. He endured many other side effects but took each day as it came. In the winter of 2007, it became apparent that his body had grown tired and was beginning to shut down. Charlie explained calmly that he knew this would happen but that one never gives up hope, always remaining open to God's plan and timetable. He was at peace with whatever God decided was right for him.

Charlie entered the beautiful Hospice Center, where he received wonderful care, and he loved all those who served him there with such tenderness. Charlie had been intimately involved with the concept of Hospice care for more than thirty years and had supported my involvement with them, both as a nurse and member of the board of directors since its inception.

Charlie retreated more and more into that quiet time that belongs to God alone, yet he wanted me to be with him at all times. I guess a sixty-two-year committed Christian marriage has a great deal to say about that. All of his sons came to visit as well as daughters-in-law and grandchildren. His first great-grandchild was born that year, and we displayed a large photo of Charles William Lewis V where Charlie could look at it all day long. The baby looked just like Charlie did as a baby! Isn't God awesome?

One son and his family lived in town, and their son, who is a medical student, was very close to his grandfather. He came by every day when he left work at Mayo and spent hours with him. The time, love, and affection showered on this wonderful young man in the past by his grandfather was now being returned in full measure, pressed down and overflowing during his last days on earth. Scripture prepares our hearts and minds so well for these understandings, if only we have the eyes to see.

Four days before he died, Charlie closed his eyes and retreated even deeper into that sleep that rewards us with the peace that defies all understanding and that comes directly from the God Charlie loved all his life. His grandson had gone to Atlanta to visit friends for a few days, and when he returned, he relieved me for an overnight stay by his grandfather's bed. Charlie was aware but not responsive anymore, but he smiled whenever this grandson spoke to him. He had waited for his return.

When I came in early the next morning, I sent my grandson home to get some rest. Charlie died quietly as I read the first seven verses of Psalm 95 to him. I held his hand in mine, and he gently went to be with the Lord he had served for so long and had been waiting to see. Charlie was eighty-six years old when he came face-to-face with his Lord and Savior.

I am so thankful for the time God gave us together, and for the time his sons were able to spend with him, alone, during those last days. I am more than sure that each of them in their own way shared their hearts with Charlie and thanked him for loving all of them so well.

I could not weep. I was so happy for him to be with the Lord, and yet, after all the things that must be attended to following the death of a loved one, I felt very much alone. Several weeks later, I was suddenly awakened during the night to see Charlie standing at the foot of my bed. His hands were outstretched, reaching toward me lovingly, and he had the biggest grin on his face, which seemed to be glowing with joy. I held out my arms to him in return, and he simply vanished from my view. I cried tears of great joy and thanked God for this wonderful gift. I pray that others will receive a moment like this when their loved one leaves as well. Ours is an awesome God. He cannot be outdone in generosity, and although I had heard stories from others in the past similar to this, it was magnificent to have this gift from God that was all my own.

Levi

"In that moment, God Himself gave the words to me"

Susie Russell

When Trudy first contacted me about contributing a story for her second book, I just smiled. The first thought I had was, *Look what the Lord has done!* God had wanted her first book, *Glimpses of Heaven: True Stories of Hope and Peace at the End of Life's Journey*, published, and He had seen to it.

As a former volunteer coordinator with a Hospice program, I am more than familiar with the wondrous experiences God allows His people to have as they are preparing to go home to Him. We recognize His handiwork over and over again and are never surprised by what He allows us to see firsthand. When I was reading Trudy's note, my immediate thought was of a former volunteer, a gentleman I knew through his work with us. His name was Levi, and he had been diagnosed with a terminal illness years earlier and now he was dying. He was Jewish, although I am not

sure if he was mostly "culturally" Jewish or "spiritually"
so. I only say that because this was a thought of mine on
the day I visited with him. Over the years, many friends
of mine who are Jewish explained the difference.

Levi was declining rapidly, and a colleague reminded
me that if I wanted to see him again, I needed to visit him
at the Hospice Center that day.

I remember praying for him and for his soul many times
over the years as I worked with him and wondering if
he knew his Lord in a personal way. On the way to his
room, I prayed that the Lord would open an opportunity
for me to speak with him about His love. I asked that I be
shown how to encourage him to seek God's peace, if he
had not done so, as he approached his final days and possibly hours of life. I silently asked, *Lord, help me to witness
to and pray with this wonderfully caring man in a way that will
bring comfort and peace to his heart and soul and not offend him
in any way. Please help me.*

Little did I know that just on the other side of his door,
waiting to greet me, was the answer and direction to my
prayer. I knocked softly, opening the door an inch or two,
just wide enough to be able to let him know it was me and
ask his permission to enter. He recognized me immediately
and smiled, inviting me in. When I opened the door fully, I
found myself staring at the most beautiful poster I had ever
seen, which he had received from a friend. It was one of
those oversized posters mounted on the wall right next to
his bed, and written in the center in large bold script was the
word *shalom*. Behind the word *shalom* was the word *peace*,
starting at the top of the poster, in smaller letters, written
in rows over and over again. It was breathtaking.

Even before I greeted him, I said, "Levi, that poster is so
beautiful, it takes my breath away!" He agreed and shared
with me that it was a gift from a wonderful friend. We
spoke for just a short time that day because I could see he
was very tired. I shared with him again, as I had done so

many other times in the past, how fortunate I was to have met him and thanked him for his loving concern for the patients he had served over many years. Before leaving, I asked him if it would be all right for me to say a prayer with him before I left. He simply smiled and answered, "Certainly." I picked up his hand in mine and began my prayer by thanking the God of Abraham, Isaac, and Jacob for the peace He was giving to Levi here and now. The words just flowed so easily, and I knew why.

I had never begun a prayer in that manner before. It was not even a way I had heard others begin a prayer in the past. I do know for certain that in that moment, God Himself gave the words to me. I thanked Him for Levi's life and for his love of others and God and asked Him to fill Levi with the shalom peace that came only from Him. It was a short prayer, and I ended it, "In Your holy name, amen." Levi smiled peacefully and answered, "Amen." I kissed him on the forehead, and he returned my gesture with a hug. Then I left his room, closing the door quietly behind me. It was to be my last visit with him. Levi died days later in peace and comfort, the way God wanted him to.

Even today, as I think back on that moment, I remember feeling the peace that surpasses all understanding that the Bible speaks about so often, and I thanked the Lord again and again for that sacred time He allowed me to spend with Levi. God wanted Levi to be at peace. He wanted him to feel and to know love as he went home to Him. God uses all of us to be His hands and feet, His heart and hands if only we will listen. He welcomes us right into the center of His will for others. He straightens the path before us and gives us exactly what He wants us to share with others. We are indeed the blessed children of our heavenly Father.

Later on when sharing this story with a Jewish friend, my friend told me that she opens her prayers in like manner and was certain that the prayer God had given to me was one that would have brought Levi great comfort. Levi was born in Jesus's own tradition: Judaism. He had struggled to imitate Him and follow in His footsteps all his life. He was longing for that peace Jesus spoke about, and he served hundreds of Hospice patients with the same gentle kindness that Jesus reflected. I was so grateful that God called me to pray with His child.

Todd

"The Lord works in mysterious ways"

Bonnie Tingley

Todd was a three-day-old newborn baby with dark, straight hair and beautiful blue eyes. His color was dusky, unlike the normal pink coloring you would expect in a newborn. It was the first telltale sign of his heart problem; the doctor quickly discovered that Todd had a hypoplastic heart. A hypoplastic heart is one in which the two lower chambers of the heart fail to form, which left Todd with a weak heart that simply could not continue to beat much longer.

His mom, Mary, and his dad, Jim, had decided to take him home, where they felt they could give him the tenderest loving care possible. They were determined to do all they could for their new little one, even though this would be a short and bittersweet experience for them. Their pediatrician had done a wonderful job preparing both Mary and Jim for what they could expect from a medical standpoint. Emotionally and spiritually, these decisions would be between them, their baby, and God. When we spoke about how long Todd might live, the doctors told us maybe two weeks. I had to admit to myself that this was going to be a challenging situation, most especially for this loving family, and then for me personally, as the mother of young children myself.

The first order of business was to assist the family in settling into their new roles as parents and caregivers of a terminally ill baby. On their first day home, everyone was more than weary. Mary and Jim had processed a great deal of information all at once and were feeling overwhelmed, but even in such difficult circumstances, they were determined to make everything as peaceful and happy as possible. This was a strong, committed couple, and they shared with me their prayers for little Todd and for themselves. I must admit it was heart-wrenching to see them lovingly care for and attend to his every need. Nurses are supposed to remain somewhat detached in caring for patients and their families, but there are times when that is not possible, and this was surely one of them.

Time was moving quickly, and if the doctor was right, they had only about two weeks to enjoy their baby and build lasting memories to cherish for their future. I wanted to help them make the most of the short time left with this precious child. Jim was a problem solver and wanted to be able to handle and resolve every new challenge as circumstances with their baby changed. He did it all extraordinarily well. Jim's business had given him whatever time off he and his family needed, which made this time even more sacred and special. God surrounds us with Himself in the hearts and faces of those He puts on this journey with us. We are never alone.

I returned the next day to check on the baby and his family and to see how their first night went. Todd seemed to be developing colic, and when he cried, his mother worried even more, because the crying was faint and really exhausted him. I thought of my own two babies who had difficult times with colic, and how unfair this added problem seemed to be for this little one. This precious family, in my opinion, had enough difficult circumstances to handle without dealing with the pain of colic. But as with many circumstances in life, this one was not under our control. I knew, and so did this young couple, that God had the ultimate answer to everything and we had to trust Him. We prayed hard about each new challenge as it arose and trusted God to pave the way before us, making it smooth.

Mary had obtained some medication for the colic from her doctor, but she did not feel it was helping very much. She and Jim wanted, above all else, for Todd to be peaceful. I asked Mary to call me later in the afternoon if the colic started again, and I suggested she try the medication then, closer to his feeding time. When I made a call later that day to check on Todd, I was surprised to hear her say, "I've found a very different solution that is working much better than the medication." It seems that just as the colic started up, Jim had decided to help Mary by cleaning up a bit around the house, and he began to run the vacuum cleaner. The sound of the vacuum cleaner seemed to soothe Todd, and he stopped crying immediately whenever he heard it. Mary said every time Jim turned off the vacuum, Todd would begin to cry again, but when Jim restarted it, the crying would stop.

A vacuum cleaner turned out to be both a solution and a strange answer to prayer. Many of my visits were made with the vacuum cleaner running, but it was music to everyone's ears. The young couple called it a real blessing, and one that none of us would have come up with on our own. Todd was unable to cry as the time left to him drew to a close and he became weaker and weaker. The soothing sound of the vacuum cleaner allowed him the restful sleep he was in such need of. Who but God alone would have come up with such an answer? It is in times like these when you realize that God is tapping you on the shoulder and saying, "It is I." You need to look no further than the still, small voice God uses to speak to us all the time. Peter asks the Master, "To whom shall we go? You have the words of eternal life" (John 6:68). Scripture is alive to us in all the challenges of our daily lives. This is why we call it the living Bible. It is presenting God's Word and direction to us in ever-expanding and enlightened ways.

Mom and Dad spent more and more time just loving and holding Todd now. He seemed to need less food and more cuddling. Cradling him in their arms, rocking him, singing to him, and just loving him is the way they spent their last days with him. Family prayers centered on asking Jesus to take this little one home to heaven peacefully and gently where he would be made whole.

Todd died in a little over two weeks, just as the doctor had said. The colic turned out to be the biggest obstacle threatening their resolve to give loving care to their little son and enable him to have a gentle death. What a strange turn of events to find a vacuum cleaner as the source of a blessing. Mary and Jim had deep faith and were able to trust the Lord to give them the strength and know-how they needed to care for their child. Although the time given to them to love Todd was short, their memories of him will last for a lifetime. The Lord certainly works in mysterious ways.

Leonard

"I just want to believe"

Trudy Harris

Leonard came to the Hospice Center because he had no family in the vicinity to care for him at home. Leonard was divorced with children, and he was dying of AIDS. He wanted so badly to understand it all, to understand his life, his pain, his sorrow, and his illness and what it all meant for his future. Leonard had an engaging personality and had been a Hospice volunteer for years, making a wonderful difference in the lives of many people. Now that he was in the Hospice Center, he was looking for a way to be helpful again.

One day when he saw me outside his room, he asked what my role was at Hospice. I explained that I was a nurse, having worked in Hospice care for more than twenty years, but that I now headed the Foundation for Caring, which raised the funds necessary to serve the needs of every patient who needed our special kind of care.

He understood the business of my office and staff and asked if he could help me a few times during the week, to make the days go by faster. Of course, I said yes immediately. I knew this would lead to something, but what it was I did not yet know. I was open to anything God had in mind for Leonard and for us.

A few times a week, he stopped at my office door and asked how he could help. I would put him at the round table next to my desk, and he would stuff envelopes, organize filing, stamp envelopes, and address invitations. No job was beneath him, and he greatly enjoyed being helpful to me. In my office, Leonard often heard conversations with families who had questions about Hospice care and all that it offered. Sometimes, too, he heard a prayer requested and said on the spot for someone in need. He began to recognize and understand the healing dimension of spiritual care within a Hospice program, in a way I felt God really wanted him to know.

He absorbed it all and often asked questions about God, the reality of Him, if he could learn to love Him, and how we come to believe in Him in the first place. Leonard was of Jewish background, but he shared with me that he did not go to temple and thought of himself as culturally Jewish but not religiously so. When he asked questions about my faith, I simply told him about the Jesus of his own Jewish ancestry, the one Christians believe to be the promised Messiah of the Old Testament. I told him how Jesus had died for the sins of all humankind, once and for all, and wanted nothing more than for us to love and follow Him and to be with Him in heaven when our earthly lives were over. I answered all his questions as he asked them, and we enjoyed our time together immensely.

I do not think I ever met anyone who had a greater desire to know God than Leonard did. I often thought how wonderful it was that Leonard wanted so badly to know the God who loved him so much and who had loved him first. He had a great thirst for God, and I wondered what Jesus would have done if he'd met Leonard during His travels. Would He invite him to follow Him? Would He have supper with him and introduce him to Peter, James, and John? I really think He would, don't you? This is what Catholics often refer to as "baptism of desire," and at times like this, we leave the person's soul in the hands of Jesus, trusting in the fact that we have introduced the person to Jesus and leave the rest to Him.

Leonard declined over the next several months and was less able to walk the short distance to my office. Now, he arrived by wheelchair. Sometimes he was too weak to get there on his own, so a volunteer would assist him. Sometimes he was able to do things for me. Sometimes he only wanted to be there, to sit quietly, watching the comings and goings of my staff. He would look at the cross hanging on the wall, the hand-stitched pastel angel (a gift from one of my patients), or the stained-glass cross handmade for me by a developmentally delayed friend. He would ask again about their meaning or purpose and listen carefully to anyone who answered him.

Many of the staff came to know Leonard well, and each time they stopped in or just passed by his door, they would pray for him to receive God's peace and the awareness that he was loved and forgiven. I cannot begin to imagine how many prayers were said on his behalf, but to say he was covered in prayer would be an understatement.

By now, Leonard was in his room more and more, declining every day, very weak, but always happy for me to stop by for a hug or a quick prayer. One day, I stepped into his room to find him sitting alone in a corner chair, crying. As I walked toward him, he stood up with great difficulty but with lots of determination to hug me. As I put my arms around him, he buried his face in my neck and cried so hard I thought my heart would break. We remained in that position for a long time.

"I just want to believe so much," he said. "I just want to believe."

"Your desire to know Jesus pleases His heart greatly," I said to him. The Scripture verse "I will never forsake you or abandon you" (Heb. 13:5) came to my mind in that moment, and I shared it with Leonard. Taking a beautiful phrase from a nurse friend of mine, I said, "I have a very large umbrella filled with faith—get under here with me, and I will walk this way with you." We stood for the longest time together, arms around each other, and if you could not recognize Jesus in the center of that circle, then you would not recognize Him anywhere you encountered Him. That was the last time I saw Leonard alive.

I know for certain that Christ visited Leonard often, through every person He put in his life to care for and serve him and love him. We can never fully understand another's pain. Some of us have life experiences that make it so hard for us to trust, accept, and reconcile an understanding of and faith in God. God, however, never lets us go. He holds on to us and keeps pursuing us even when we think we cannot find Him. I am sure He stayed with Leonard until he was safely home.

Rudy

"How can anyone not believe in God when they see how beautiful my vegetable garden is?"

Trudy Harris

During more than fifteen years of my work in Hospice care, there was one person who was at my side morning, noon, and night. Edry came to work with me as a temp when my assistant, Madeleine, became ill. Edry stayed with me with the utmost dedication and love for the last fifteen years of my career. She awakened me each morning with a call to outline the day and all its appointments. Hers was the first voice my husband heard as he passed the phone to me. A more dedicated, compassionate professional could not be found anywhere, and I treasure the friendship we share to this day.

Edry had been married to Rudy for more than fifty years, and they had one lovely daughter, Lynn, a son-in-law, Jess, whom they loved very much, and two grandchildren, Jessica and Michael, who were their hopes and dreams for the future. Rudy had met Edry when she was a basketball star at her high school, and they married a short time later. To say that Edry's family fell in love with Rudy would be a great understatement. Her two brothers, Arnold and Hugh, thought the world of him, and her sisters, Joyce, Jean, Margie, and Belva Lee, saw him as a big brother/ father figure all rolled into one.

Rudy was a true southern gentleman in every sense of the word, believing that women should always be treated with dignity and respect (even when they did not deserve it). His mother died when he was eight years old, which fostered a self-sufficient spirit within him. He developed a close relationship with his aunt May, who would prove to be his guide later in life. It is always interesting to look back to see how God intervened in our lives through others. He chooses those He knows will teach us and guide us through the rough times we encounter. He never leaves us orphans but stays with us all our lives.

Rudy was a kind and generous man and so creative. He built two of his own homes and about 90 percent of all the furniture in them in the workshop behind his house. He hand carved the headboard in the master bedroom, staining and hand rubbing it until it looked like glass. It is beautiful to this day. Dining room tables, end tables, stools, chairs, and headboards and footboards for other bedrooms were just a few of the masterful creations he made with tender loving care. He loved his workshop, which was every man's dream, and it held the latest tools for every job imaginable. It had a twelve-foot worktable, windows on all four sides for maximum lighting, a TV, A/C, radio, and chairs for the many visitors who came by.

Family members and friends often requested such things as microwave carts, end tables, trays, and diaper chests when a new baby was on the way. The Adirondack tables and chairs he made for my family grace the deck of my son's home in Charlotte, North Carolina, some fifteen years after he made them. Rudy loved his gray 1989 F-150 Ford truck, which transported the completed gifts to their new homes. There is something very special about a carpenter whose hands and tools bring joy to others—truly one of God's most generous gifts, and when used for others, as Rudy's were, they fulfill Jesus's wish that we love and take care of each other, as Rudy did.

Rudy's gardening talents were endless, and he won several awards for the largest and most beautiful tomatoes in the area. "How can anyone not believe in God when they see how beautiful my vegetable garden is?" he would say. "The beans, peas, tomatoes, and cucumbers are just so perfect." Rudy grew prize-winning roses and gladiolas that looked for all the world like velvet, and he loved the sunflowers best, because their faces always followed the sun. He marveled at the beauty and perfection that God put into everything his hands touched, and he in turn shared their bounty with others. He canned vegetables, taking cases of mason jars to his daughter and son-in-law when they were away at college. His generosity knew no bounds and came naturally to him. He, in turn, was loved and admired for it.

I tell you all about Rudy's accomplishments because they reflect the heart of the man God created him to be. Alone early in life, he learned to find joy in the simple things and to create beauty where none existed before. He used his God-given talents to bring happiness to others, and I believe he tried to do that until the day he died. Men of his generation were not long on talking; his deeds spoke for him. He fixed many a door, window, or roof for someone, and he did it quietly. Never one to draw attention to himself, he represented the person we hear about in Scripture who was told to do good in secret, and our heavenly Father, who sees in secret, will reward him.

Rudy was an active Christian all his life, but in later years he could no longer get to church. "You don't have to go to church to know and believe in God," he would say. "The way you treat your family, especially the children and your neighbor, is a much better way of showing it."

The years passed by quickly while Edry continued to be my hands and feet in Hospice work. Rudy was more than generous, allowing her to spend entirely too many ten-hour days helping the Hospice Center become the success it is today. Many an evening I heard her on the phone with Rudy, planning a late-night supper, and he did not complain but supported her and the important work she was doing.

Rudy was slowing down over the years and really began to decline at age eighty-four, having trouble regulating his blood pressure; he was always cold and fatigued easily. When the circulation in our bodies begins to slow down, everything is affected, and so it was with Rudy. He was admitted into a local medical center for seven days, during which his daughter called me. She had worked with Hospice for several years, and her husband was the Hospice chaplain. They felt Rudy was beginning to decline quickly, which was hard for all of them. He had always been the one they leaned on and trusted; it hardly seemed possible that he would die so quickly.

As familiar as Edry was with all the signs and symptoms of approaching death, she did not believe this was happening for Rudy. His physician, who knew him well, recommended Hospice care, and Rudy was admitted into the Hospice Center the next day. When I stopped by for a visit, he was happy to see me. He knew where he was and why he was there, and his eyes told me he understood everything. Visitors came from everywhere, and the family that loved him so well never left his side.

On the last day of his life, Rudy said to me, "Is Aunt May gone for the day or is she going to come back into my room?" I stepped into the hall to ask about Aunt May only to be told that she had died more than twenty years ago and had been close to Rudy after his mother died, when he was a small boy. I told Rudy she had left for the day but would see him tomorrow, which seemed to please him a great deal. He smiled and nodded his head in agreement.

God always sends the very people He knows will bring comfort and peace to His children as He draws them home to Himself. It is an amazing experience to be near many people of all ages as they are dying and to see how intimately and personally God is involved with each one of them. I knew then just how close Rudy was to going home to the God he loved and honored all his life.

Edry needed to have a break, as she had been with Rudy nonstop for days. I suggested she go home for a while, have dinner, rest, and come back to the Hospice Center later in the evening. I promised to stay the night with Rudy while she rested nearby. She was exhausted beyond all measure, but it meant everything to her to be with him when he died.

About three in the morning something or someone awakened me. I took one look at Rudy and knew it was time to call Edry. I stepped outside his door and tapped her on the shoulder; she entered the room immediately. Rudy was completely aware of her presence next to him, and as she whispered in his ear, he took three short breaths and died. Aunt May was waiting for him, I am sure. He died the way he had lived, peacefully and unafraid and with Edry, his friend for life, by his side. It does not get any sweeter than this.

Naomi

"Why is she not talking to any of us?"

Trudy Harris

Naomi had a very large, loving family, and she, their beloved mother, was sick and not going to get better. They were doctors, lawyers, housewives, brothers and sisters, nieces and nephews, and grandchildren. They never left her side in the hospital room, not even for a moment.

Naomi was as wise a woman as you could imagine, having raised many children. She loved them all fiercely and had raised them well. Strong faith was the center of their home—God came first in all things and in all ways. But these were very independent, accomplished people, accustomed to making things happen for themselves, to being able to influence and change the course of lives, laws, and so forth. Their mother's illness, however, was not one of those things that could be influenced or changed. Naomi had been diagnosed with terminal cancer, which had spread everywhere in her body, and now in her late eighties, she longed to find peace and go home to God.

"Why is she not talking to any of us?" one of her sons asked as I entered Naomi's hospital room. "She smiles and speaks to you when you come by, but she will not say a word to any of us." This wonderfully handsome, loving, accomplished son was distraught because the mother with whom he had a loving relationship was now choosing not to speak with him or any others in the family.

"What do you speak with her about when you are with her?" I asked him.

"About getting better and going home," he answered. "I tell her all the things we still want to do with her, that we need her and we love her."

"Does she speak to you at all about what is happening to her?" I asked.

"Oh no, we don't talk to her about anything like that," her son replied.

This consummate mother, who had given birth to, cradled, loved, and raised this wonderful family, was now dying. She knew it, and she knew they did as well, but they would not allow her to speak of it. "There is no way my mother is going to spend one day angry with me," her son said. "That would be a first, and it's not going to happen."

Being the oldest in the family and accustomed to being in charge, this son led his brothers and sisters to the quiet of a small waiting room, where I explained to them what was happening to their mother. This was a committed family of strong Christian men and women who knew their God and His will for their lives. This mother had been so deeply loved and depended on that life without her seemed impossible for them to comprehend. However, when they realized that her not speaking to them was a direct result of their not allowing her to share her journey with them, they all did an enlightened and immediate about-face.

Death is a journey, and we can walk it accompanied by others or we can walk it alone. When we are dying and able to talk about this final journey, we feel a sense of peace and accomplishment and a sense of being loved and understood. When we are unable to share this experience with those we love the most, we feel abandoned and alone. This family did not want their mother to feel alone, even for a minute, and they did not want to feel on the outside of her love for them either.

The oldest son reentered his mother's room. He spent the rest of the evening talking with her about her plans, where she wanted to be, and what this, her final journey, was all about. Naomi told her children she wanted to go home immediately, to be in her own bed, surrounded by her family.

I never stepped into Naomi's house again when grandchildren were not in her bed, holding her hand and loving her, or when good food was not cooking on the stove, whether she could enjoy it or not. It brought her great comfort to know that life was continuing as usual for those she loved. The Scripture verse that says, "Her children rise up and praise her" (Prov. 31:28) came vividly to my mind.

Naomi had a storybook ending to a life filled with meaning and purpose, one that had been Christ-centered from the earliest days. She died quietly at home a few weeks later with her entire extended family by her side. They stayed with her until they knew she was safely in heaven, receiving the eternal reward that God had promised her.

Father Jack

"Yes, I remember you well"

Trudy Harris

Father Jack was a rather rotund figure in his mid-sixties, all smiles with a tender and patient demeanor as he sat during the children's Mass each week at Christ the King Church. As each child stood to read the Old and New Testament readings and a psalm as part of the service, Father Jack would nod in approval and smile. The children always looked his way when they finished and were grateful for his approval and his smile. He was the kindest of all creatures, gentle with the children and others and called by God to minister to His people. Father Jack did it with great faith and love.

Years passed, and after my children graduated from grade school, I did not see him for a long time. When I met up with him many years later, he had been diagnosed with cancer of the throat, which brought with it challenges of the very hardest kind for Father Jack. For a priest called to ministry and preaching, removal of the voice box has to be the worst kind of suffering. Learning to swallow, to eat, to sip liquids, and to enjoy life again was not going to be easy. To prayerfully redefine what God was asking him to do in a completely new way was an enormous challenge.

One test after another, one treatment or surgery after another, and the cancer and its aftermath were taking their toll on Father Jack in every way possible. If ever the devil likes to tempt us to give up, to be weary, to feel dejected and sad, it is in times like these, and it was no less so for Father Jack.

I heard one day that Father Jack was back in the hospital, so while visiting a Hospice patient there, I stopped by to see him. He smiled as I entered his room, and as I began to introduce myself, he patted my hand, acknowledging wordlessly that he remembered who I was. What do you say when you visit a true messenger of Jesus Christ who now has no voice? What words do you use? I quickly begged the Holy Spirit for inspiration, and He answered me immediately in a way I did not anticipate. I sat down on the small step stool next to the chair he was sitting in and said, "It has always been a dream of mine to go to confession to a priest who could not talk back to me or tell me things that I need to do differently, so here goes." I promptly confessed my sins, asking God to forgive me, through this sweet and suffering priest. Father Jack patted me gently on my hand and pointed to the Rosary he was holding, indicating I was to say the prayers contained therein. A tear fell down his cheek, and as I stood up to leave, no words were spoken.

Years later while shopping at the mall, I saw him again looking very well and walking toward his car. I rolled down my window and called out to him. "You won't remember me," I said, "but while you were in the hospital and could not speak, I stopped by and gave my confession to you." Placing his finger over the device in his throat that helped him to speak, he smiled and said, "Yes, I remember you well." It was a very tender moment, and one for which I will always be grateful.

Time passed, and Father Jack continued to be well and ministered to the different communities God had chosen for him, just as he had done before. He was as much loved as he had ever been, if not more.

Years later, a call came to my office late one afternoon from the church rectory. Father Jack was very ill and in need of our Hospice care. The staff at the church requested I come by that day. The Irish nuns who had been serving God faithfully with Father Jack for many years were lovingly caring for him in his room at the church's rectory. The pastor of the parish, Monsignor Mortimer Danaher, wanted only the best care for his longtime friend. He had invited Father Jack to live at his house so he could see to it. Father Jack was attended to around the clock not only by the church staff and his brother priests but also by many of his parishioners to whom he had ministered for many years and who held him in great affection.

Father Jack was declining rapidly, and on many afternoons I would stop by to check on him as I ended my day. On one particular visit, a dear friend of Father Jack's and mine, Carol Kelly, greeted me as I entered his room. She had been a parishioner for many years, and she was relieving the staff for a few hours by sitting with him. She was, according to Monsignor Danaher, one of the most devoted and faithful friends Father Jack had, and she spent a good deal of time seeing to his needs. The love and devotion Father Jack had shared all his priestly life was coming back to him one-hundred-fold, by people just like Carol.

When I looked at Father Jack, I knew that I could make him a great deal more comfortable if only I had some extra help and some big strong arms to lift him with me. At just that moment, I heard a knock on the door and in walked Father Daniel Logan, a fellow Irish priest and friend of many years. Father Jack greeted him with, "Hello, Danny boy," reflecting a long and wonderful relationship between the two of them. God sent just the right person at this moment to help us, as men did not come any stronger than Father Logan. He did everything I asked of him, lifting and turning Father Jack, making him immediately more comfortable, and Carol kidded with him about taking orders so well from a woman. He was careful in turning Father Jack so as not to hurt him, and he did it all with ease and a big smile. He wanted nothing more than to have his friend as peaceful and comfortable as he could possibly get him. It was lost on none of us that God had sent Father Logan at the exact time we needed him, to help his friend and us. The look of gratitude on Father Jack's face said it all.

Father Jack continued to be wonderfully cared for by his fellow priests and the nuns with whom he had taught, as well as by those friends he had ministered to and cared about all his life. He died easily and well, and I am certain that Jesus said to him as he entered heaven, "Welcome home, My good and faithful servant, and see what has been prepared for you from the beginning of time." Father Jack was now receiving the eternal reward promised to him by Jesus Himself. What you give away in kindness all your life comes back to you in good measure, pressed down and overflowing, just as the Scriptures tell us.

Ed

*"Pray for us sinners, now and at
the hour of our death"*

Nancy M. Powers

I have often wondered about the supernatural beings who surround us every day. So much so that I have frequently prayed that God would one day lift the veil between heaven and earth, so I could see them in some way. On March 6, 2001, at approximately 6:00 p.m., I believe God gave me just that—a glimpse of heaven.

One of nine children, Ed O'Neill was born on August 2, 1919, to parents who kept the family together by running a bakery in Jacksonville, Florida. Ed played baseball in high school and was drafted into the minor leagues, but unfortunately Uncle Sam got to him first, so Ed joined the navy. In New York City, Ed met the love of his life, a feisty Irish girl nicknamed Sheila. She was also in the navy, as a WAVE. Sheila and Ed married in 1945, and after the war ended, they celebrated together with the rest of the world in Times Square, where the famous photograph of "the kiss" was taken. Those two young lovers in the photo easily could have been Ed and Sheila.

They had two daughters while living in NYC and one winter too many. Ed, a southern boy, decided he was ready to go home. He would often tell the story of walking home from work one night, stopping frequently along the way just to keep warm. He and his wife moved their small family back to Ed's hometown of Jacksonville, where they had four more girls. The last one lived for only three days.

Ed found himself in a home filled with women but did not seem to mind a bit, and if he had ever hoped for a boy, he never mentioned it. The family of seven lived in a 1,300-square-foot house, with three small bedrooms and only one and a half baths. The five girls shared two bedrooms and somehow survived sharing only one bathroom. By today's standards, the house would be considered small for a family that size, but it never felt small to the O'Neills. Ed loved having friends over and entertained often. The house was always filled with good cheer and fellowship.

When Sheila was experiencing a difficult pregnancy with her sixth child, Ed would often come home from work, pack the five girls into the car, and take them to the beach. This outing gave Sheila a much-deserved break and cooled the girls off from a day in their small, non–air-conditioned home. Sheila preferred the quiet to the cool.

This sixth little one never came home from the hospital. Losing the child was an enormous sadness for all of them, but one they accepted with the same faith that always sustained them. God had a different plan for this baby, and Sheila and Ed guided their young family with this understanding.

Ed worked for IBM, Setzer's grocery store, and finally Pantry Pride, where he was the comptroller. He had an extraordinary work ethic that he instilled in all his girls. He was never the type to brag about anything, and he lived his life quietly. He was always there for his God, family, and friends, in that order. Whenever his girls came to him for advice, he would take his time to think the situation over carefully and then quietly share his thoughts. He never jumped for the quick and easy answer; instead, his advice was always steady and strong.

Ed was a man of deep and abiding faith, attending church regularly all his life. He brought his family up in the faith, putting each of them through years of Catholic schooling. Even when Ed lost the ability to form cohesive thoughts, he continued to recite the prayers he had prayed throughout his life.

In 1997, after several health scares and recoveries, Ed was showing early symptoms of Parkinson's disease. He hid it from everyone for as long as he could, becoming quieter and more introspective every day. The family noticed that he was being more forgetful and talking less. When his disease progressed so much that he could no longer drive safely, his daughters happily drove him everywhere. No matter how frail his memory and speech became, Ed wanted to be sure that when his daughters were off work and spending time with him, it was a "legitimate" day off and they were not shirking their responsibilities elsewhere.

Even as Ed's physical capabilities diminished, he had a quiet twinkle in his eyes and a knowing smile whenever his wife, Sheila, was near him. If this was not the understanding love Jesus spoke about so often in Scripture, then I have not seen it anywhere else in this life.

Ed's signs and symptoms indicated with each passing day that he was becoming weaker, and he was no longer able to bounce back as he once had after a serious setback. But he was totally at peace with God and his faith. He had walked and talked with God all of his life, prayed faithfully to Him, and had fought the "good fight" as St. Paul tells us in Scripture. And although he did not want to leave his beloved Sheila and his daughters, he knew that God was beckoning him home, and he was ready to meet Him.

Two of his daughters—Mollie and Justine—Sheila, and I were sitting with Ed one afternoon. It was a quiet moment as his daughters rested on either side of his bed. They held his hands while Mollie prayed silently. In a moment of grace, Mollie asked her sister Justine if she would like to pray with her. Justine agreed, and they began to pray together. Many people misunderstand the Rosary, which is so familiar to Catholics. While it appears to be nothing more than several prayers repeated over and over again, it is actually a reflection on the life of Jesus Christ. The first part of the "Hail Mary" comes from the Scripture verse when Mary visits her elderly cousin Elizabeth, who says, "Rejoice, oh highly favored daughter, the Lord is with you. Blessed are you among women" (Luke 1:42). In the second half of the prayer, we simply ask Jesus's mother, chosen by God the Father to bear His Son, to pray for us. The Rosary begins with the Apostle's Creed, a prayer said in Christian denominations throughout the world for centuries. The Rosary also includes the "Our Father," repeated five times, and the "Glory Be to the Father," an ancient Christian prayer, repeated five times.

Sheila got up from her chair at the foot of Ed's bed and joined her daughters in saying the prayers so comforting and familiar to her family. As they continued to pray together, tears of comfort, sadness, and joy rolled down their cheeks. Ed's breathing slowed peacefully to the rhythm of the Rosary prayers. He joined his spirit to his family's spirit, and together they said the ending of the Hail Mary. "Holy Mary, Mother of God, pray for us sinners, now and at the hour of our death, amen."

In those moments, the tears flowed from everyone, as we all knew Ed's time was very near. When we were all joined together in prayer, Ed was at peace; when we paused or stopped, Ed waited for us. The moment was so spiritually beautiful that it could only have been a gift directly from God Himself.

One by one, gliding in like angels, the nurses and aides who had compassionately taken care of all of Ed's needs surrounded him at the foot of his bed. Their presence gave recognition to every heavenly angel that was in the room with us, ready to take Ed home to heaven.

Sheila gently whispered into her husband's ear the words of love that only fifty-five years of marriage can express. His daughter Justine kissed him and blessed him with her tears, and Mollie told him how much everyone loved him. They watched as once and for all he opened his eyes and smiled. He was looking at them as he took his last breath on this earthly journey back to the Father who had created him. It was a very holy moment for a very holy man.

That day and every day, Ed sees the face of God. That day and today, in my heart, I know I witnessed a "glimpse of heaven." God had answered my prayer.

Anna

"Trudy, it's only about love"

Trudy Harris

Anna's husband had died in our Hospice program. She wanted to honor his memory in some special way, and she came to speak with me about it. "He loved the outdoors," she said, "nature and the beautiful things in the garden." We were just beginning to build the Hospice Center at that time, and we planned to have it surrounded by beautiful gardens, so she decided on one garden, in a special corner spot, that she liked the best. And so this garden, just outside my office window, was named in honor of her beloved husband. It became Anna's custom to visit me often and to stay for a while in his special garden.

Anna, apparently, was not very well herself. She said nothing, of course—that was not her way—but her breathing came in "short pants" and her color was not good. She struggled getting in and out of the car, but she visited me often, and we became fast friends. She had a crusty way about her—tough, no nonsense, "say it like it is"—and we enjoyed our time together. She asked to meet in my office frequently, to split a tuna salad sandwich with chips and a soft drink, and the menu never varied.

Every time Anna visited me, she would empty a large manila folder on my desk, reflecting a large financial portfolio. "Don't you want to look at this? It's all yours," she would say with a big smile. At first, I had no idea what she meant and was taken aback that she trusted me with such personal information. Slowly but surely, over time, she told me many things about herself, including the fact that she had no children. She had helped many in her family financially over a long period of time, and now she wanted to make a difference for others in a completely new way. My role as president of the Hospice Foundation for Caring gave me the opportunity to make friends with many people who more often than not came to understand and value the work of our organization. They wanted to ensure that we would always be able to care for those who needed our help. Anna felt strongly about wanting to help us care for terminally ill children and adults who needed us at this very special time in their lives. She was happy with the financial decision she had made in this regard and met with her financial advisor, laying out her plans to do so.

Anna and I became good friends, talking often, sharing lunch, and trusting each other well. During this period, I noticed how much harder it was for her to move about, to walk, to talk, no less drive. One day while visiting with her in her home, I told her my foundation hat was now off and my nurse's cap was firmly in place. I explained carefully to her that I was seeing a definite change and decline in her health, and it was time for her to allow Hospice to help her to live fully each of the remaining days that God had planned for her. To my astonishment, she agreed with me immediately. Trust meant everything to Anna, and she really trusted me.

The Hospice team came in to care for her, and because her living conditions were such that the bedrooms were all located upstairs, we put twenty-four-hour nursing care in place for her safety. Anna met any discussion regarding a move to the Hospice Center with anger and threats, and to say we went toe-to-toe at times would be an understatement. I cared deeply for Anna. She knew it, she believed it, she trusted it, and better than anything else, she knew it had nothing to do with her money or her gift plans for our Hospice program.

We spoke often about heaven and the afterlife, which she believed in. She was not sure about all the intimate details of God, but she believed in Him, trusted in Him, and wanted to understand Him better. Her time was running out, and she sensed she had work to do.

Anna was spending most of her time in bed now and declining more each day. She was pleased that she had been able to finalize most of her plans for the future of the Hospice programs and the people she cared about most. She called her financial advisor and asked him to meet with us so he could understand the needs as well as she did. On top of all the other gifts she had given to Hospice, she wanted desperately to set up a special fund to serve the more than eighty terminally ill and dying children cared for in our Hospice program.

Anna opened the door to a new awareness of the fact that children die in Hospice programs every day throughout the United States. Although she was unable to do what she wanted for the children's program herself, the family of a man who had met her only once established a very large pediatric endowment a few years later. Anna had planted the seeds God had asked her to, and she would have been thrilled to know that these little ones would be cared for now through their generosity.

A little while before Anna's death, something, it seemed, had not yet been settled in her heart. I do believe, from all she said and did over a week's period of time, that she was having many intense visits with God and was no doubt talking with Him about many things. She was learning to understand from God's point of view and reconciling unfinished business between them. During the last week of her life, when I visited each day, Anna would lie quietly, hearing my voice praying with her but never reflecting by word or action that she knew I was there. She did this for three full days, taking nothing in and not responding in any way. I arrived on the fourth day, early in the morning, and spoke softly to her with my face close to hers. She opened her eyes wide and smiled a very tender and beautiful smile.

"Trudy," she said, "it's only about love, do you know that? Only about love, nothing more, nothing less." Her face reflected a radiance and peace I had not seen in her before. She then simply closed her eyes. Jesus tells us in Scripture to set our hearts on the greater gifts. I believe Anna did just that in those last three days of rest and found her gifts when she arrived in heaven.

God stays with each one of us from the moment we are conceived until the moment we leave our earthly bodies. He is making Himself known to us in many ways and through all kinds of people and experiences. He asks us to be like Him, to follow His example, and to be His disciples, and He is teaching us how, even when we do not know He is near. He tells us, "Be still, and know that I am God" (Ps. 46:10 NIV). He was with Anna during all those years that she was being so good to others, but when she became silent, she was able to see and hear His heart speaking to her. It is good for us to be still and listen.

Richard

"What should I tell her? What will I say?"

Trudy Harris

Richard was a forty-two-year-old, handsome, successful corporate attorney in our community. He arrived at our small, newly established Hospice office late in the afternoon and simply asked if he could speak to someone. This was very early in the Hospice movement in our area, when little to nothing was known about end-of-life care and no one really spoke about dying.

Since I was the only nurse in the office at the time, I invited him to my desk to talk. He was pale and clearly shaken, and I knew immediately that he was about to share something very serious. Richard's company scheduled annual physicals for their employees, and Richard had just met with the physician to review all of his test results. As he was telling me this, he started and stopped several times, trying hard to hide his tears and shock, but he finally spoke of the diagnosis the physician had shared with him. He had multiple malignant tumors in his lungs, which were inoperable due to size and location, giving Richard a prognosis of four to six months. All Richard could speak about was his wife and two small children. All he could express was the deep, painful understanding that their lives would be lived without his love and guidance. "What should I do?" he asked. "What should I tell her? What will I say?"

The heartache expressed by this young husband and father was beyond belief, and I found myself without the words to comfort him. I simply got up and walked around my desk to hold him. He sobbed uncontrollably for a long, long time, expressing his enormous sorrow in leaving his family. Not once in the entire conversation did Richard speak of or ask about his own welfare. Not once did he express fear for himself or for what might lie ahead for him as far as suffering was concerned. Granted, he was in shock, but often in circumstances as cruel as this one, our true natures surface quickly and it usually is "all about me." Richard's nature was obviously one of being "other centered" and thinking of his family's future and their long-term welfare and not his own.

After a long period of time, Richard composed himself and simply asked what Hospice could do for him and his family to make the time left to them as good as it could possibly be. I explained to him that he would have a nurse, a social worker, a volunteer, a chaplain, and a medical director all intimately involved in his day-to-day care. He began to cry again. "You all must be angels," he said. "I think God is going to help us all through this time by sending us His angels, like you, in disguise." He spoke then of his Christian faith and belief in Jesus Christ. We spoke about the promises Jesus gave to us before He died: that He would go before us and prepare a place for us so that we could be with Him forever. We spoke about Jesus telling us He would never leave us orphans but remain with us always, until the end of time. I reminded him about heaven as our eternal reward and about the fact that God always has a plan for our loved ones and us, even when we do not want it or understand it. We spoke about the angels, whom he felt would be helping him and his family now and after he was gone.

I was only four years older than Richard and married with young sons at the time he was in my care. I could not even begin to imagine the pain and sorrow he was experiencing. As we prayed together, I begged God to be with him, to comfort and console him and to give him the courage I knew it would take to walk the path laid out before him.

By now, a few hours had passed, and Richard the lawyer had reappeared. He had "reviewed the facts of the case," he had "asked all the right questions," and he had "researched his options and made some decisions." He had the answers now that he needed to move forward, reflecting the skills that he relied on in the world of "man's law" in his everyday work.

But there was more now, much more, and Richard knew it. The "law" he could rely on most heavily now was not man's law but God's. God and God alone would guide Richard's next steps. He was the one who would direct him from here on out and prepare him not only for his future but also for the future of his family. How good it was for Richard and his family that he had relied on God's direction all his life, which made it possible for him now to trust that he was safe, even in these circumstances. He exuded the confidence that only comes from loving and trusting God and nothing more.

When Richard finally stood up, we embraced, and then he left, standing tall and going home to share the news with his wife and children. Richard became a Hospice patient within the week and lived his remaining days to the fullest. His young family surrounded him, and he was cared for by those he referred to as his "angel group." He died peacefully four months later, with his wife and children by his side.

I stayed in touch with this young family for quite a while after Richard died. They were comforted in their loss by the fact that they had loved him well, had wonderful memories to sustain them, and knew of his love for them. His children grew into fine young adults and reflected the deep and abiding faith that had sustained their parents during a painful time. His was a life very well lived.

Joni

"Mama, Jesus has me by the hand.
I have to go now"

Annie Rini

One could always find a vase full of day-old roses in varying colors and sizes next to Joni's hospital bed. Sam, one of this precious five-year-old's most ardent admirers, would bring her roses from a local floral shop on his way to work at the children's hospital. Yes, even at five years of age, Joni knew very clearly what her likes and dislikes were. In addition to flowers, Joni enjoyed painting, crayons, the "play lady," and riding her IV pole like a skateboard down the hall of the hospital each night before going to bed. Riding "the pole" was a distraction, meant to help smooth the transition between getting ready for bed and saying goodbye to her mother, a single mom who had to get home to care for her older child. While Pam, Joni's mother, always lamented that she had to choose which daughter to spend time with, she knew she couldn't be in two places at once, so in the early evening she would leave Joni to us and go home to be with her other child.

Joni had leukemia, the type that typically has less chance of survival, especially in those days before the advent of bone marrow transplants, which provide improved chances of recovery. At the time of her diagnosis, most children with this disease spent a good portion of their time receiving treatment in the hospital as opposed to in a clinic as is done today. The hospital quickly became a home away from home, if such a thing were possible, for Joni and children like her.

I came to know Joni and her family very well, as I had the privilege of caring for her during my three-to-eleven shift as a pediatric nurse. The beauty of the evening shift on a pediatric ward is that the commotion of the seven-to-three shift is over. Children are fed dinner, given their medications, and then readied for bed, much like at home. More time could be spent with children at the hospital bedside, sneaking a few precious minutes to read a bedtime story, watch a TV show, or comfort a child whose parents had gone home for the night after a long day at the hospital.

Joni, although just five years old, amazed me with her humor and spiritual maturity. Whenever her minister would come to visit, which he did often, he would end his visit by asking, "Joni, would you like to pray with me?" Joni readily obliged, closing her eyes and bowing her head in prayer. She would then begin to pray for her family, her friends, everyone except for herself. When finished with her prayer, she would always end their visit with, "Thank you, preacher, see you next time." What manners for a child so young and so sick.

As her illness progressed despite heroic efforts to keep her disease in remission, Joni developed complications. One night she bled into her brain from low blood counts. Her mother rushed to her bedside and lay across her body, begging her not to die. Joni rallied that night and eventually fully recovered from the effects of the bleed, leaving her with miraculous, full function of her brain, body, and spirit. She returned to her usual self, charming and cheering other patients, parents, and staff. Unfortunately, this was for a very limited amount of time.

Joni's disease returned with a vengeance, and her mother decided that whatever time she had left should be spent at home. Her real home, not her hospital home. Joni was kept comfortable and was able to play with her older sister and enjoy being with her family once again. She eventually became less and less responsive as the disease took its toll on her young body, and she spent more time sleeping than she did awake. Her mother struggled with how to give permission to her little girl to die. Staff had spoken to her about a child's ability to stay alive long past the appointed time, until they felt it "permissible" to die and leave their parents and family behind. Joni, it seemed, was very patient.

As Joni declined, Pam came to the realization, albeit reluctantly, that Joni was waiting for her. Waiting for her to give her permission to let go of her earthly life and to go on to heaven. One evening before Thanksgiving, Pam was rocking Joni, who had been completely unresponsive for several days. She leaned down and whispered into Joni's ear, "Honey, it's okay now. Your sister and I are going to be all right. When you feel Jesus is ready to take you, you can go." Minutes passed, and Joni remained still. Suddenly, she opened her eyes wide. She looked up at Pam and clearly said, "Mama, He's here. Jesus has me by the hand. I have to go now." She smiled, the smile that everyone came to know as "Joni's smile," and took her last breath. Through her tears, Pam smiled too.

Pam spoke at her daughter's funeral. One can only imagine how difficult this was as a mother preceded in death by a young child, but she wanted very much to share Joni's last words. She wanted all of us to know where Joni had gone and with whom.

I have thought about Joni at least once or twice a year for the past twenty-five years. Her parting words continue to inspire me and those I tell of her journey. I believe it is truly through Joni's experience that I was able to share not only her life but also her gift of childlike faith and hope. Jesus's words remind us that unless we become as little children, we shall not enter the kingdom of heaven. I look forward to seeing Joni again one day.

Darleen

*"God entered into that quiet through the
simplicity and grace of Father O'Flynn"*

Trudy Harris

Darleen and her husband, William, lived in a beautiful
country club setting with their home overlooking a lake
and a golf course. You could spend hours wandering upstairs and down and never get to see all the changing views
from every window in the house.

They had raised two sons there, both of whom lived a
good distance away now. They had taken care of Darleen's
mother for many years, in her own private suite of rooms,
until she died just a few years before. Since then, it had
been just the two of them enjoying their retirement years
together.

Darleen had a malignant brain tumor, and although she
was still quite young and active in her early seventies, she
was going to die of this disease. William and Darleen were
a quiet, "stay to themselves" couple. They did not socialize
much and did not have a network of friends on which to

rely now. They were comfortable with that and enjoyed being just the two of them.

Keeping Darleen comfortable and pain free was William's only concern, and over many an early morning cup of coffee, he and I would speak about how to do that. Her diagnosis made her prone to severe headaches and seizure activity, which oral medication had kept under control until now. However, at 3:00 a.m. one morning, William called me in a panic. Darleen was having a major seizure that was lasting much longer than any she had experienced in the past. He asked if I would come over right away. I lived about two minutes away, so I told him I would be right there and to call 911 immediately. And soon, there I was in my pajamas and bathrobe at 3:00 a.m., giving Darleen emergency medication to control her seizure.

When the ambulance arrived to attend to Darleen, the EMT looked askance as I reviewed her condition with him, telling him of the meds I had given her and why and directing him to the hospital where she was to be admitted. It took him a moment to put the pieces of the puzzle together and realize that Hospice care happens at all hours of the day and night. Whatever needs to be done for the patient's safety and well-being happens on the spot, and Hospice nurses are known to stay one step ahead of everything so as not to have crisis mentality for the patient or family. William and I laughed for years after about the sheer humor involved in a Hospice nurse attending a patient in the middle of the night in her pajamas and bathrobe, and the look on the EMT's face when he arrived.

With the right medications given intravenously, Darleen's seizures were immediately under control. She was discharged from the hospital to her home one day later. Her decline was more evident with every passing day, and she wanted to be with William in her own home.

Darleen and William did not have a church community to which they currently belonged. They had belonged to one in the past, but the time involved in caring for her mother had kept them from church longer than they wanted to remember. They asked if I knew anyone, a priest or a minister, who would come and pray with Darleen. I was so happy they asked.

Father Seamus O'Flynn, my close and faithful friend who always came at a moment's notice and who comforted William years later as he was dying, stopped by for his first visit. After that first visit, he made it his duty to visit Darleen often, ministering to her just as Jesus would have done. The sight of them sitting together, head to head, in meaningful conversation and prayer has never left me. The comfort it brought to her soul was beautiful to see, and it comforted William's heart as well. On one such occasion, Darleen asked if Father O'Flynn would conduct a graveside service for her when the time came. He agreed immediately, and they reviewed all of her favorite Scriptures to plan the day.

Darleen died in her beautiful home with her husband and her sons nearby, the way they had always lived those many years ago, quietly and together.

Father O'Flynn arrived at the cemetery early on the morning of Darleen's service. I kidded with him about knowing all of his Scriptures by heart, which of course he did, not only because he read them often but also because he lived them every day.

God makes Himself known to us in the ways He knows will be easiest for us to receive Him. He knows us better than we will ever know ourselves. Darleen and William were quiet people. They lived their lives with simplicity and grace, and God entered into that quiet through the simplicity and grace of Father O'Flynn. There were no horns and whistles, no loud voices, just quiet, gentle peace and love. It reminded us all what Jesus is truly about.

Tom

"I have to tell you a story, and I hope you don't think I'm crazy"

Ede Pearson Huston

I had been a Hospice nurse for many years when my fifty-eight-year-old husband, Tom, was diagnosed with cancer of the left adrenal gland. You would think my years of experience would make me comfortable with the terminal phase of an illness and that the dying process would seem natural to me. But that is never the case with a loved one. All of our insights and experience go out the window, and we become simply the patient's spouse. All the objectivity and professionalism exhibited with the patients and families we have served become lost in the emotions of having our life partner die. Suddenly we are on the other side of the caring spectrum, and it feels awkward and comfortable at the same time. We learn to depend on others for support and trust their knowledge in a whole new way.

We are, after all is said and done, just like everyone else, very human.

When you are a Hospice nurse, you see and hear many things that you would not ordinarily experience in a hospital or home nursing. Hospice nursing teaches you to listen carefully to what your patient is and is not saying. Body language—long, thoughtful pauses and expressions— become very important to watch for. Many people express themselves in actions that are new for them, such as being suddenly open and anxious to share with you when that had not been their previous nature. This often reflects new understandings and experiences that the patient is having and suddenly wants to share.

The last few weeks of Tom's life were difficult following his surgery. He was one of those people who had always been stoic, reserved, and not given to a great deal of conversation. He did not require much pain medication, or any other meds for that matter, so his mind was clear and remained that way until the very end of his life.

One afternoon, I had to leave him for a short period of time to run errands. He was fully alert, so I felt comfortable doing so. I asked him to stay in bed while I was gone and said that I would be back just as soon as I could. He was comfortable with my leaving and had enough on and around his bed to keep him busy for the little time I would be away.

When I arrived at home with all my errands accomplished, I found Tom in bed, crying. I asked him if he was in pain or if there was anything I could do for him. Tom replied, "No," but then he continued to say, "I have to tell you a story, and I hope you don't think I'm crazy when I do." I assured him I would not and asked him to tell me whatever he had on his mind. He looked at me and smiled. "While you were gone," he said, "my mother came to visit me. My mother was here in this room, she sat there on the cedar chest at the foot of my bed. She looked really pretty, just like she used to. She held out her hand to me and smiled. She said, 'Come on home with me, Tom, it's all right.'"

I asked Tom if he was fearful about what had happened while I was gone. He said, "No, it was actually kind of nice, it was pretty much okay." From then on, Tom was happy knowing that when he died, his mother would be waiting for him and that he would be reunited with her in heaven.

Tom had been a very spiritual man all of his life. He was peaceful and trusting in his faith and knew where he was going when he died. He continued to receive Holy Communion at home throughout his illness, which was brought faithfully to him by the Eucharist minister from our church. Tom had made his peace with God and was prepared to meet his Creator when He called him home. We had been very comfortable speaking about spiritual matters together for a long time, and it brought us both a great deal of comfort.

As a Hospice nurse, I could recognize the signs and symptoms of approaching death; it was no different now with Tom, as my husband. This last piece of the puzzle was now in place. Knowing that he had seen his mother and that she was waiting for him gave me great peace as well. I was enormously grateful to all my nursing friends who made this last period in Tom's and my life comforted and supported. When God says He will prepare the way for us, this is what He is referring to. He knows exactly what we each need in order to find peace in the circumstances of our lives. He allows us to experience that which He knows will give us that peace so we are no longer afraid.

Matthew

"Today you will be with me in Paradise"

Bonnie Tingley

I was working as a PRN nurse at the local Hospice in our city. This means I worked in the place of a patient's regular nurse, covering their day so they could accomplish other necessary tasks, paperwork, and so forth. I received a call from the office and was assigned to visit another nurse's patient. His name was Matthew; he was my age, forty-three, and dying of lymphoma. Matthew's wife was named Lynn, and they had two wonderful children together. Matthew was struggling with questions about the existence of God, Jesus, the Holy Spirit, and heaven. All things pertaining to God and the afterlife were a big challenge for him, and he wanted to talk about all of it. His regular nurse said she knew I was a lot more comfortable dealing with "spiritual matters" than she was, and she wanted me to talk to Matthew. I gathered myself together, obtained his medical information, and headed out to meet him at his home.

I prayed a quiet prayer in the car that I would say the right things to this patient and that the Holy Spirit would be present. Hospice nurses can't possibly have all the answers on their own. It was the practice of most, if not all of us, to pray before, during, and after every visit. Matthew was waiting for me, as his nurse had told him that I would be more comfortable answering his questions than she was. This was a huge task, which I knew I was not prepared to handle without God's help, so I was counting on Him to get me through this assignment.

Matthew had previously refused an invitation from his minister to visit with him. He lost no time in testing my faith as he began his questioning. "How do you know the gospel is really true and not a bunch of made-up stories?" he asked. That led me to address the issues of faith and trust. Matthew said he just could not accept anything he could not see and verify. He was a realist, after all, and needed proof. A thought popped into my head, and I began to tell him about a book I had just finished reading, *This Present Darkness* by Frank Peretti. I explained to Matthew that Peretti had been able to write a fiction book allowing us to look through a window into a realm that we just are not able to see with our earthly eyes. Peretti had raised the shade, so to speak, and given us a peek into the spiritual realm that was all around us. I told Matthew I would send the book out with his regular nurse, and even if he did not believe, he might enjoy reading an action-packed book about the battle of angels and demons. He thought that would be a good read, and said he looked forward to being able to check out the book for himself. He agreed to have me return after he finished the book so that we could talk again.

Several weeks passed, and Matthew's regular nurse contacted me to say that he was ready to have me visit again. He had finished the book and wanted to talk. This time, I found Matthew in bed and in a much weaker state than before. He told me he had really enjoyed the story but was still struggling with his inability to believe. We talked about his family and his worry about what was going to happen to them after he died. I felt a nudge from the Holy Spirit and asked Matthew if he would like to have me pray for him. He readily agreed. I laid hands on him and began to pray. Feeling a flood of love pour out for him, I heard him begin to cry then sob. I continued gently asking the Lord to minister to Matthew and to let him know how much He loved him. "Please fill him with the peace that only You can give," I prayed.

When we finished praying, he looked up at me, both crying and laughing at the same time. He looked straight at my face and said, "I thought you would go home and pray for me. I never expected you to pray like that, right here and now." Matthew said that he was overwhelmed by the whole experience, which was obviously very new for him, and he needed to think about everything that had just happened. Matthew thanked me and asked for my home phone number, which I gave to him.

Later in the week, I received a call from his wife, Lynn, asking me if I would feel comfortable coming out to the house to pray with her and Matthew. It seemed he had gotten a bit better after he and I had prayed that day, and the Holy Spirit was teaching him in a whole new and wonderful way. I asked if it was all right for my husband Terry to come with me, as we prayed often together as a couple. Lynn was grateful and readily agreed. Terry and I visited with them one evening, and together we prayed for them and their family. The Lord seemed to repeat the same process I had experienced earlier with Matthew; this time also with Lynn. We watched as a flood of tears and peace descended on both of them. They expressed to us the enormous gratitude they felt because we were there with them. As Hospice nurses, we do not aggressively share our own beliefs. We recognize the physical, emotional, and spiritual dimensions and needs of the dying patients in our care, and we respond when we are asked to. We respond prayerfully, with grace and humility as they seek and find, often at the end of their lives, the Lord who has always been with them.

Matthew's nurse shared with me that as time passed, his day-to-day living improved for about a month. This short period of improvement was followed by a rapid decline. His nurse relayed that Matthew had asked his minister to visit with him and decided to accept Jesus Christ as his Lord and Savior. He died peacefully a short time later. His wife was relieved, knowing that Matthew had found his way home to God.

On the day Jesus died, He turned to the thief on His right and said to him, "Today you will be with me in Paradise" (Luke 23:43). At times like these, the Scriptures come alive before our very eyes and we hear them again as if for the first time. Ours is an awesome God.

Marsha

"Will you please pray the 23rd Psalm with me?"

Bonnie Tingley

I had spent the whole day seeing many of my patients and was now finished and on my way home. I was on call for the night, which meant that any patient who called with any kind of need would be either spoken to or seen by me. I had just left the office when the first call came in. The patient's name was Marsha, and her family was asking if I could visit her right away. They were very concerned, as they sensed things had been changing quickly in the last few hours. I made my way through the evening traffic and found her home quickly and without any difficulty, which was a good thing, since I had not seen this patient before. When I stepped inside, the whole family greeted me with gratitude and a sense of urgency. Marsha's sisters and children were with her.

When I stepped into her bedroom, I found a lovely woman in her late sixties lying snugly in her bed. Marsha had been admitted into the Hospice program only a short time earlier, and I did not have a great deal of information about her. I knew she was dying of lung cancer, but at this moment, she appeared to me to have some time left to her.

I have learned over the years to listen closely to both the patient and the family at times like this. They often know best what the patient is trying to say or do, and if you listen carefully to them, you can meet whatever need they are expressing. The family was concerned because they felt things were changing quickly and that her time left on earth was very short. I checked her vital signs of blood pressure, pulse, and respirations and found that although they were not strong, they were not as weak as you would expect if her life were truly ending at any moment.

Her family was sitting closely all around her and asked her quietly what she would like them to do for her, and she whispered in reply, "Will you please pray the 23rd Psalm with me?" I was invited into the circle of the family, and everyone began to pray.

> The LORD is my Shepherd;
>   I shall not want.
> He makes me to lie down in green pastures;
>   He leads me beside the still waters.

I had my eyes open and was watching Marsha closely. She looked immediately more relaxed and peaceful with every word spoken. Her family continued on:

> He restores my soul;
>   He leads me in the paths of righteousness
>   For His name's sake.
> Yea, though I walk through the valley of the
>   shadow of death,
>   I will fear no evil;
>   for You are with me.

There was a gentle but noticeable change in Marsha, and a wonderful sense of peace filled the room. In that instant, I realized that she had just let go of her spirit and was now walking into heaven with her Lord.

> Your rod and Your staff, they comfort me.
> You prepare a table before me in the presence of
> my enemies.

In my mind I could see Marsha being led to the table of the Lord with all its goodness set out for her to see. All the things she had not been able to eat or enjoy for many months were now available to her without restriction.

> You anoint my head with oil;
> My cup runs over.
> Surely goodness and mercy shall follow me
> All the days of my life;
> And I will dwell in the house of the LORD
> Forever. (NKJV)

Marsha was indeed dwelling in the house of the Lord. Her family was happy and relieved that her death had been so merciful and told me she had been a Christian for many years. The family felt blessed to have been able to pray her into heaven. It was miraculous to see the way Marsha was able to give up her spirit to the Lord she knew and loved so well.

It occurred to me on my drive home that Jesus had given up His spirit to His heavenly Father just as Marsha had given hers over to the Son. His presence was palpable to everyone in that room. He is indeed the Good Shepherd who leads us safely home.

Kenneth

"I am dying, honey, but do my children know?"

Trudy Harris

Kenneth was in his mid-seventies and had lost his wife to cancer years earlier. He was a happy-go-lucky kind of man who had wonderful, loving, protective children.

He was a strong, faith-filled Christian who had raised his children the same way he was raised, following in the example and footsteps of Jesus Christ. Frequently on my visits with Kenneth, a son or daughter would be in attendance, some who lived far away and others who lived close by. Kenneth was never alone. His children attended to his every need, making sure his home was beautifully kept the way he always wanted it to be, cooking his favorite foods, and staying close.

Kenneth was told several months earlier that he had stomach cancer, and everyone in his family knew of it as well. They also understood that he had terminated treatment, since it could no longer make a difference in his condition or add time to his life.

Although everyone knew of his diagnosis, no one spoke of it with him, so Kenneth and I spoke of it with each other. One day he asked me what lay ahead for him, how long I thought it would be before he would die, and how I thought his children would handle losing him. His concern was for them, and although he knew that their faith would hold them in good stead, he hated the fact that his leaving would cause them pain. They had experienced a lot of sadness years earlier when their mom had died. They really loved each other, and Kenneth had always been the kind of dad who approved of his children and did not hold back from telling them so. He knew his approval would be a part of him that would never leave them, and he was grateful now that he had learned that lesson well from his wife.

His faith in Jesus gave Kenneth the peace, spoken about so often in the Bible, that defies all human understanding. This peace was fully understood by Kenneth and his children. When they spoke with me about their dad and what was happening to him, they were in full agreement that he faced this diagnosis in the same way he had faced everything in life, with dignity and grace. His children remembered that, when their mom had died several years earlier, Kenneth had taught them by example to face every difficulty in life with Christ by their side. It surely had made them good, strong men and women.

But his children somehow could not bring themselves to speak to their father about his diagnosis and impending death. It seemed to me that although he was not physically by himself on this journey, he was still very much alone. Kenneth understood his children's great love for him and their desire to protect him, but his illness was not some secret of which he was unaware. Essentially, death is a journey, and when we take a journey, we usually talk about it with our loved ones and our friends. We make plans together and share our thoughts and concerns with those we love. Sharing makes things easier and allows meaningful conversations to take place in ways that often have not happened before.

One day, while I was visiting with Kenneth in his bedroom, he looked up at me and said, "I am dying, honey, but do my children know?" As he said this, he pointed to the living room, where his children were gathered.

"Yes," I replied, "they do know, they just don't think you do." He smiled at first and then actually laughed aloud. The very thought that he was dying and might not know it hit a funny bone with him. He had always been a realist, spoke frankly about things as he saw them to his children, and could not believe that they really thought he did not know about his own dying. He asked me to have them join him in his bedroom "right now."

When his children gathered in the room, he smiled at them and said, "I am dying, you know, and it feels like I'm doing it all by myself because you won't talk with me about it. It's okay for me to die. I'm ready to go, and I'm not afraid. I hate to leave you, but I know where I'm going, and I'll be with your mother there and am looking forward to seeing her again. This is what we've talked about all our lives, going home to God and our eternal reward when He says it's time, right?"

The room was silent for just a moment—no one even blinked. Then all of a sudden they moved forward as one and piled onto the bed with him. They hugged, kissed, laughed, and cried, sons and daughters, several grandchildren, and the dog. It was one beautiful sight. It was what Kenneth had been waiting for.

Things changed from that day forward. This loving father and his children comforted one another and rejoiced together in the short time that was left to them. This new openness gave his children the opportunity to say everything to him now while he was still with them rather than regretting not having done so after his death.

There are so many lessons to be learned from this family. Life is to be lived to the fullest for all the days God gives to us. No man is an island unto himself; the journey is meant to be shared.

Helen

"I had to learn how to forgive"

Trudy Harris

Helen was a woman in her early sixties who had gone to many doctors, one after another, trying to discover why she was tired all the time, why she had a persistent cough, and why she was losing weight. For many months the doctors could not give a diagnosis, and she and her family were very frustrated.

She had been married to her husband, Jack, for more than forty years, some of which he spent away in the service while she stayed home and raised their children alone. To say that Helen was an angry woman is a huge understatement. Quick-tempered and often sarcastic, Helen approached most of life with an attitude that obviously covered a great deal of pain. I have always been drawn to cranky, ornery people and believe that most are good, just hurting.

By the time I met Helen, she had been diagnosed with cancer of the lung. It was inoperable, and although she had radiation treatments to reduce the size of her tumors and give her some relief, she knew she would not get better. Her prognosis was six months or less, but Helen decided she was not going anywhere anytime soon. She dug in her heels—hard. Most people decide to "let go" when their hearts and souls and bodies are at peace. We are much more than a disease-filled body when we are dying. We are made in the image and likeness of God and therefore consist of body, soul, mind, and spirit. When these things are warring against each other, there is no peace; when things are resolved, peace finds its way to us.

In a short time, Helen and I became close friends, and she shared many things with me. It seems she had discovered that her husband had been unfaithful to her while he was in the service more than thirty years ago. It was something she could never forgive nor forget. Her entire outlook on life, her relationships both inside and outside of the family, were deeply marred by her anger and unforgiving spirit. Here was Helen, dying of an unrelenting cancer of the lung, with a husband and children surrounding her at all times, and yet she spent most of her time punishing the husband who had betrayed her all those years ago.

It was more than evident that Helen would never find peace and go to God with ease or grace if she did not come to an understanding of God and His unconditional love. Her oncologist, who was a kind and quiet Jewish man, was mystified as Helen outlived even the most generous of predictions related to her deadly disease. "I am just not ready yet," she would say to him whenever he asked how she was doing. Even when he said that he was surprised she had lived this long with her terminal diagnosis, she would simply repeat, "I'm just not ready yet."

Helen knew she had work to do and that not addressing her own personal issues was holding her from moving on. The work of forgiveness can be difficult, especially if it is not practiced in the everyday challenges God allows to come our way throughout our lives. It becomes a weighty bag we carry around on our back, cutting into the creases of our hearts and influencing everything in our lives. Anger and unforgiveness that become a way of life literally eat away at our souls and blind us to the abundant life Jesus wants us all to have.

More than a year went by, and ever so slowly but surely the little prayers Helen and I said together when I visited began to make a difference for her. She spoke to me often about the pain she suffered when discovering her husband's infidelity. Helen had been so young at the time, raising their children alone, trying to make ends meet and trusting him so. Her wound was very deep, and alone she could not heal it.

We spoke about Jesus and the way He loves us, and when we repeated the "Our Father" together, the words took on new meaning for her. "Forgive us our trespasses as we forgive those who trespass against us" took on a completely new sound that Helen had not been listening for in the past.

By God's grace alone, Helen came to the understanding that forgiveness is not a feeling but rather a decision we make when faced with difficult challenges in life. By God's grace as well, she did not hold it against herself that it had taken her so long to come to this understanding. She simply decided to speak to her husband and to forgive him. When you see grace in action, there is no question in your mind about what you are seeing; you know it and it is beautiful.

The effect this had not only on Helen but also on the entire family was profound. The tension and anxiety that had been literally palpable for most of their lives was gone. Now, sweetness expressed with soft and loving eyes took its place, and it was for me nothing short of a miracle.

I was with her at her next doctor's appointment. When the doctor walked into the room, he looked at her with a surprised expression and said, "What has happened to you?"

"I had work to do," Helen said. "I had to learn to forgive, and I have."

He was speechless and could only smile at the happy and radiant expression in her eyes.

Now that Helen's heart was at peace, she could begin to "let go," understanding that this meant she was going to die very soon. I was preparing to take a short sabbatical from Hospice nursing, and I knew she did not have much time left. On my last visit with her, I got up on the bed with her and told her how much I had loved being her nurse and her friend but that it was now her time to go on to God. One of her daughters was traveling from out of town to visit her that night. Helen knew she was a very high-strung and nervous girl, unable to cope with too much confusion and emotion. "It will be much easier for your daughter, Helen, if you are in heaven before she gets here, so why don't you just go on in now." With that, I kissed her gently good-bye and left for home.

I had been gone from their house for less than an hour when her husband called. He said that Helen had simply closed her eyes when I left, placed her hands in his, and died.

Helen's prognosis had been six months or less, but she lived for more than two and a half years. She knew with certainty that God had given her the extra time to correct the wrongs in her life, to forgive her husband, to give her family and herself peace, and to go on to heaven. God was so patient with her, giving her all the time she needed to find her way. He absolutely does not want to lose even one but wants all of us to come home to Him in safety and peace.

Cathy

"The greatest of these is love"

Bonnie Tingley

Judith was a single mother with two daughters. The youngest, Cathy, was a precious six-year-old suffering the end stages of leukemia. During one of my early visits, as we were getting to know each other, Cathy shared with me the drawing that she had made with her crayons. The picture was one of a grassy hill complete with flowers, two stick figures, one taller than the other, holding hands. A third stick figure was crossing a long, rainbow-like bridge. That figure was about three-quarters of the way across the bridge. Perched above the small stick figure was a bright yellow sun. The bridge seemed to end in the blue sky and clouds. Cathy left the picture on the table and bounded out of the room to play. Judith shared with me that Cathy had been drawing this and many other similar pictures, in different forms, as her illness progressed. Judith explained that one of the early pictures had the three stick figures standing together at the foot of the bridge looking into the sky. We talked about her "bridge of life" and what that picture meant to Judith. Her mother saw this picture as a way for Cathy to express the fact that she saw her time on earth coming to an end.

Visits with Cathy and her family continued for over a month. On one visit, Judith told me that Cathy had been playing on the neighborhood playground just a short distance from her house. One day, Cathy had come running into the house bursting with excitement over what had just happened to her while she was swinging. "Mom," she said, "you won't believe who came to see me." When Judith inquired as to whom the visitor was, Cathy replied, "Jesus came to visit me and told me He would come for me soon."

Judith and I had a quiet talk, discussing the changes she was beginning to see and the things to watch for as Cathy got closer to her time of dying. People, especially children, always know better than those around them when time is growing short. You learn to listen to them more than to anyone else. We also spoke about Judith's Christian faith and what a comfort it was to her and her children, now more than ever. She shared how hard Cathy's death was going to be for her and for Cathy's grandmother as well. Her grandmother loved her so much and was actively involved in her day-to-day care.

About two weeks after that visit, as I was heading home, a strong feeling came over me that I needed to visit Cathy right away. There is no way to explain such sudden insights that seem to come to you out of the blue except to realize that the Holy Spirit is prompting you and it is a good time to listen. In Hospice nursing, you learn to do that quickly. I made the decision to stop and check on Cathy and her family right away, and soon pulled up in front of the house and knocked on the door.

Judith opened the door and ushered me in. "I was just getting ready to call you." She said that things seemed to be changing quickly, as she had been having a hard time waking Cathy up and it was time for her pain medicine. Judith was rightfully concerned that Cathy would awaken in pain, which often happens when pain medication is skipped. When I looked at this precious little six-year-old, I knew for certain that she was about to die. A large lump rose in my throat, and for a moment I was unable to speak. I prayed quickly for the Lord to give me the right things to say and do for this child and her very loving mother.

I asked Judith to sit in the rocking chair next to Cathy's bed. Just as she sat down, I placed Cathy in her arms. She began, ever so gently, to rock her back and forth. I whispered to her that Cathy was very close to going into heaven now. She started to cry softly but suddenly stopped and began to speak quietly to Cathy. She reminded her that they had talked about this moment many times before and it was now time for her to go to heaven to be with Jesus. Judith assured her precious six-year-old daughter that she would hold her close until she was in Jesus's arms and feeling safe with Him. She then ever so gently walked her into heaven.

There was a palpable peace in that room as Cathy slowly relaxed in her mother's arms; we knew immediately that she was now safe in heaven. Judith asked her mother, who had just entered the room, if she wanted to rock Cathy. As the grandmother took her seat, Judith placed Cathy lovingly in her arms. Cathy's grandmother began to rock her back and forth; she looked tenderly at her and slowly came to the realization that Cathy was not with us anymore but safely in heaven with Jesus, just as He had promised.

Yes, there was much sadness in that room, but it was tempered with a sweet sense of peace and serenity. I had both seen and received a lesson of true love in action that day. Seeing a mother set aside her own feelings of grief to be able to give so lovingly and unselfishly to the needs of Cathy and her grandmother was overwhelming to me. I drove home wondering if under the same circumstance I could have done for my child what I had just witnessed there in that home.

As I neared my house, a picture opened in my mind's eye, and I saw a beautiful field of daisies. A little girl dressed in the sweetest white dress was running through the field, picking handfuls of white daises as she went. It was Cathy! She was no longer pale and bald but pink cheeked with beautiful, long blonde flowing hair flying in the breeze. I remembered Judith telling me that Cathy had long, beautiful, wavy hair before she had lost it to chemotherapy. I found myself feeling a sense of overwhelming joy bubbling up inside me, which I could not explain. Suddenly I realized that my Lord had given me two very special gifts that day. He had given me a true lesson of unselfish love in allowing me to see Cathy's mother and grandmother love this child into heaven. And two, He had given me a sense of true joy that did not seem appropriate under these circumstances when viewed through human eyes. True joy is of a different kind and reflects Jesus, others, and you, in that order. When you experience joy in that way, you know you have it all.

This special family and the lessons they taught me have stayed with me to this day. "So faith, hope, and love remain, these three; but the greatest of these is love" (1 Cor. 13:13).

Maureen

"Mommy is sitting on the foot of my bed right now"

Trudy Harris

Maureen was the oldest of four girls in our family. She was born following my mother's seventy-two-hour labor and developed convulsions at birth. There was never any doubt in Mom's mind that the convulsions were due to trauma to her brain during labor.

In those days, seizure activity and those who suffered from it were viewed very differently than they are today. A diagnosis of seizure disorder or epilepsy carried with it the misunderstanding that the challenges a person would face would be insurmountable, so very little was done to encourage success. Maureen, like many others, proved those misunderstandings so wrong over the years and far exceeded any expectations anyone had of her. However, growing up in a society that was lacking in understanding and expectation caused a deep wound that Maureen carried all of her life. Maureen's life was ultimately so fruitful because God was with her every step of the way, giving her the insight, know-how, and courage to excel, and she knew it.

There was only twenty months difference in our ages, so Maureen and I were very close as little children. Anne was six years and Peggy four years younger than Maureen, and they played together as she and I did. Maureen and I loved games, roller-skating, playing with dolls, and going into New York on Saturdays to shop and have lunch with Mom.

For years, Maureen and I played a game we called "Yoo-Hoo, Mrs. Goldberg." We had an old iron bed with vertical rails, and we would put our heads between the rails at bedtime and emulate the popular radio show *The Goldbergs*. Mrs. Goldberg and her neighbor, Mrs. Bloom, would lean out of their tenement windows and call to each other every morning, "Yoo-Hoo, Mrs. Bloom. Yoo-Hoo, Mrs. Goldberg."

I was second in age, and from the time the four girls could stay at home when our parents went out, I was put "in charge," a place I hated being. This circumstance caused a deep wound in both me and Maureen. It was not until Maureen was dying that we finally found the healing for which we both had always longed. Growing up in circumstances like this caused Maureen to fight her way to the top and to prove herself in everything she did. And she did so in spades.

Maureen and I were in the same class all through grade school, and the thought that I was responsible to quietly watch out for her was hard for her to bear. My dad taught me never to be embarrassed by anything that happened during a petite mal episode but to always be tender and kind with her. I know it was by God's grace alone that I was able to do that, because when you are young, everything embarrasses you. Maureen in turn would run to protect me whenever a school bully was trying to hurt me. She was fearless on my behalf. I loved her dearly all my life and she me, but she was not able to reflect that love because of the very natural resentments she developed because of her early experiences in life.

Early on, Mom and Dad read every book, visited every doctor and hospital, and tried everything suggested to them in the hopes that Maureen would do well in life. Mom left no stone unturned on her behalf, and if you have ever seen a mother tiger with her cub, you would be looking at our mother.

Tears came easily and on a regular basis in frustration and heartache, but in the end, Maureen established herself as her very own person. She was the most widely read and well traveled among us and always felt she was born on the wrong continent, because she loved Europe so much. She excelled at everything she did, traveling to her beloved Ireland more times than anyone we ever knew. She found God everywhere in her travels, visited Him in the cathedrals of Europe and in the quiet of a tiny, thatched-roof cottage in Ireland. God's presence was, for Maureen, in everything of beauty in the outside world, and she rejoiced in it.

Our parents prayed together daily, and there was never any doubt on whom they relied for guidance and strength. By divine inspiration alone, my parents decided that it would be best if Maureen could go away to school on her own when she finished grade school. There she would be able to develop her very own distinctive skills and interests. This decision did not come easily, but Mom believed, given the right chances, that Maureen would succeed beyond anything she ever dreamed. Mom never believed what the doctors said about Maureen's abilities or her future; she knew better. Through sheer determination and prayer, Maureen attended the well-known Blessed Sacrament Academy in Goshen, New York. The children of diplomats from all over the world attended this beautiful school in the mountains of upstate New York. She loved every minute of it, and it was there that she first met people of other countries and cultures.

Maureen had been on anticonvulsive medications for the first eighteen years of her life and hated the way they made her feel "different." There was concern that without them she would have convulsions, which, in the end, did not prove to be true for her. When she graduated from high school, Maureen threw her meds down the commode, saying she never needed them in the first place, and for her that seemed true. She never had a seizure again in her life. Many children who have seizures in early childhood outgrow them after adolescence. Others who develop seizures later in life seem to need medication for much longer. About fifty million Americans have this syndrome and live very happy, productive, and successful lives. Medicine has indeed come a long way.

In the interim, Maureen fell deeply in love with a young man whose family fled Austria when Hitler was invading. They loved each other dearly and in the purest sense of the word, and although they never married, they remained close and loving friends all their lives.

Maureen sailed to Bermuda on her own in her early twenties, where she met her future husband, a young man from England. She sailed on the SS *United States* to meet him in England to be married a short time later. Her entire family of parents, sisters, aunts and uncles, and friends were there to see her off. Although this marriage was never a love match on either side, his desire to marry an American girl and her desire to live and travel in Europe were both met for them during the next seven years. She had adventure in her soul.

Maureen and her husband eventually moved back to the States, working in Las Vegas and Atlanta as hotel managers, with Maureen filling in at every needed spot—front desk, night auditor, whatever it took to have things well run. When her husband left her after seven years, Maureen was heartbroken. Although the marriage was not a love match, there had been happy times. He took their only car with him, leaving Maureen without one. Peggy and her husband, Jimmy, bought her a new one and put a big red bow on it, which brought her tears of joy and gratitude. They were with her during this difficult period of time, which meant everything to her.

All through her life, Maureen clung to her faith like someone who knew that God was always with her. She would often say that the whole world can let you down, but God never will. She prayed morning and night for guidance, the ability to forgive, and the happiness she longed for. God gave her many friends along the way. She loved helping people do things well, and they loved her dearly in return.

In her mid-thirties, Maureen moved to Florida with Mom and Dad, who had retired there. She was looking for a change and found it in a succession of interesting jobs over the next thirty-plus years. Dad died three years later, so she and Mom became companions, traveling to many interesting parts of the world. Maureen's life, with all its challenges, had a richness of travel, friendships, and love of books second to none. She knew well that if she completely trusted God then anything was possible, and trust she did.

Our mom by then was in her early nineties and declining ever so slowly but surely. It was during this time that Maureen was able to build her first home "to her own liking and pocketbook," as she would tell Peggy and Anne. It gave Mom much happiness to know that Maureen was in her own home, only forty-five minutes from me and just down the street from Peggy and Jimmy. We were all relieved and grateful when God took Mom home to Himself. Maureen had been her watchful guardian for many years, never sleeping until Mom's last bathroom call of the night was completed.

Maureen developed breast cancer in her late sixties and received chemotherapy for weeks following her surgery. She dealt with it with humor and grace as Peggy drove her back and forth for treatments. She and Peggy would sing "On the Road Again" as they took off for the chemo she handled so well. She went straight to work after her treatments, taking only her regular days off and never missed a day of work. She bought two beautiful wigs, and absolutely no one with whom she worked ever knew anything about her cancer.

Over many years, Anne had been extremely generous, meeting many of Maureen's financial needs in spite of the demands of her own. She was quiet in all that she did for Maureen, and both she and her husband, Bob, helped her in many ways. We each had different levels of closeness with Maureen over the years, but there have never been three women who loved a sister more or tried harder to make her life happy than we all did.

I stayed with Maureen for two weeks after her surgery, and from the first day home she was amazing. I asked her how I could help her while I was there. She said, "If you could help me clean the whole house, closets, windows, kitchen, beds, and bureau drawers, the whole works, that would be such a gift." We tackled room after room each day, moving things around to suit her. When it was finished she was thrilled. She worked harder than I did, never took a break, and never complained. She was awesome to watch just three days after her surgery. We faithfully read *The Purpose Driven Life* together each morning, and she felt it contained many answers for her, especially now.

Maureen suffered from a form of small vessel disease for years. The disease took its toll on her in later life, and it was only by God's grace that a wonderful vascular surgeon was able to help her keep her right leg six years longer than expected. But when repeat grafts no longer worked, the surgeon had to amputate her right leg. She accepted it in a way none of us could have and faced this loss, as she had so many others, with dignity and humor. She did not allow for "long faces" when it came to her leg and referred to the remaining portion as "Little Tony," reflecting a funny story our dad had told us about St. Anthony many years earlier. She delighted in the look on our faces whenever she did; it was her way of helping us all to cope.

The aftermath of this surgery—the fact that her wound would not heal—and the daily evidence of her malnutrition brought us all to a time of serious talking. While visiting one day, Maureen asked what I thought she should do, where she could go for physical therapy, and how things would be. I outlined all the options for her: having rehabilitation where she was, going to a place near home, or coming home with me. Peggy and Anne had offered to care for her in their own homes as well, but Maureen, knowing better than the rest of us what was really happening to her, said, "I'll come to your house." It was one of many little miracles that God gave to us. We were all so grateful to Him for bringing His healing touch to Maureen's heart now, if not her body. We all saw His hand up close and were happy with her decision.

We got her settled into the bed of her choosing, and it was only then that we realized the full extent of what was happening. She was no longer interested in eating and refused all her meds except those that reduced her pain. As I entered her room the first morning, she said to me, "Gertie, can you get into bed with me and just hold me?" This was absolutely the last thing Maureen would ever ask anyone to do, and my heart jumped right out of my chest. I thought it wonderful that she called me by the name she used to as a little girl. The way she said it was so tender, and although I'd hated it as a child, I was thrilled to hear her call me by that name now. I slid into bed beside her, cuddling her in my arms, and she held on to me with a hug that covered a thousand words and many, many years. It was as though, in an instant, God had healed our relationship in a way nothing else could have. She was at home, safe, secure, and knowing how much I loved her and she me.

When her swallowing became difficult and she was no longer able to take her pain meds, I called her surgeon. He suggested driving her back down to the hospital and then figuring out what to do next. I explained to him in the firmest and most patient tone I could muster that that was not going to happen. Peggy and Anne were in full agreement about not wanting to put her through any more agony. I told him, for the fourth time, that I had been in Hospice nursing for more than twenty years and that Maureen was dying. I truly believe he was shocked. He had taken great care of her for six years, yet as a surgeon he primarily saw her vascular disease and not what was happening with her as a person. He listened patiently and agreed to her Hospice admission immediately.

She was admitted into the Hospice Center within hours. There she received the most tender loving care possible. Angels, whom we call nurses, tended to her every need and reflected the compassionate heart of Jesus Christ every time she needed them. As they wheeled her in she said, "I think I am at the Ritz-Carlton." As God would have it, another miracle—the physician on staff had vast experience with amputees and appropriate pain control for them. Dr. Ruben Smith was, no doubt, exactly the physician God wanted to care for Maureen. Within hours, she was comfortable, pain free, and smiling at everyone. She knew, just as all people who are about to die know, that she was preparing for heaven. She was peaceful and unafraid as she asked to see a priest. During the ten days she was there, several priests came to visit, blessing her and giving her the Holy Eucharist. We all took turns—Peggy, Anne, and

I—spending the night with her, and she was never alone for a moment.

One day while I was with her, she said to me, "Is there room enough on this side of the bed for you to get in with me?" I jumped at the chance, another miracle. God was working in the gentlest and most mysterious ways in Maureen's heart, and I could not help but know in mine as well. We snuggled like two little children, happy as we could be. Peggy and Anne did many similar things for Maureen whenever it was their turn to be with her, and she never felt safer or more loved in her life.

We took turns staying with Maureen in an attempt to give each of us time alone with her and to give each other much-needed breaks. We slept on a small cot next to her bed, and with the bed rails up, it looked exactly like the old iron bed she and I had slept in when we were little. "Yoo-Hoo, Mrs. Bloom," I called to her one night just as we were about to go to sleep. With the most exquisite smile on her face, she turned to me and said, "Yoo-Hoo, Mrs. Goldberg." We lay smiling at each other for the longest time, and I know we'd never loved each other more than at that very moment.

Peggy wanted to spend another night with Maureen. I thought that was generous of her, since we all were tired by then, but it seemed very important to her. I knew how much she wanted to stay and say all the things sisters say to each other when one life is ending and one goes on. Anne was at Maureen's house. She had lost her own husband just three months earlier. She had planned to live with Maureen in Florida and so suffered two great losses in a matter of three months. Her heart was heavy at the thought of Maureen leaving too.

Maureen was resting peacefully when I kissed her and left for the night. Not long after, Peggy saw Maureen smiling the most beautiful and happy smile and asked her why. "Mommy is sitting at the foot of my bed right now,"

Maureen said, looking beautiful and totally at peace. She then lay back down on her pillow and fell asleep.

Peggy slept on the cot next to Maureen, and they held pinkies until they were both sound asleep. A few hours later, something suddenly awakened Peggy, and she walked over to Maureen's bed. She realized that Maureen in that moment had just walked into heaven. Peggy called the nurse to confirm what she already knew: Maureen had just received her eternal reward. She looked like an angel. When the nurse returned to the room, she placed one red, long-stemmed American Beauty rose over Maureen's heart. She had no earthly way of knowing that one long-stemmed red rose had always been a symbol of the unending love between our mom and dad. It told all of us that Maureen was in heaven now and that our parents' lifelong prayers for her were answered. Maureen was safely home with them and with the God who never left her side.

Conclusion

When Jesus said that He would always be with us, do we believe Him? Do we really think He meant it when He told us to come to Him when we are weary and we would find rest in Him? Why would He have said these things if He did not want us to understand that He never leaves us, that in one way or another He is always with us? God made us in His image and likeness and told us that we were no longer slaves but His friends. He created us to love Him and be loved by Him forever in heaven. He asks us to be His image to our hurting world.

When my sisters and I were children, our mother told us to wake up each morning thanking God the Father for the safety of the night and the brand-new day. She said to spend the entire day with Jesus, walking and talking with Him and following His example. She told us to ask the Holy Spirit to be with us as we slept and to be our teacher, our comforter, and our guide. In this way, waking or sleeping, we are always with Him. This was very sound and loving advice.

God wants us to be aware of Him at all times, morning, noon, and night, and to know that there is nothing about our lives too trivial for His concern. He asks us to be like children with Him, believing, loving, and trusting Him at all times. Think for a minute about the times you have been aware, in the smallest ways, that He is near you, that He is prompting you to understand something in a whole new way and when you just suddenly feel peaceful for no reason. Those times make you smile, make you feel safe and understood in a way that is not of this world. That is when God has let you know, in the subtlest of ways, just how close He is to you. Take a moment and thank Him—He is close enough for a whisper.

One month after Douglas died, his sister had a dream. She found herself standing in an open field of clouds and noticed him walking toward her, smiling. "You're dead," she said to him softly.

"Yes," he answered. "I have a message for you to give to my sons. Tell them I am with Jesus now and that I love them very much." How often did God comfort one of His children through a dream in the Scriptures? Didn't an angel appear to Joseph, telling him to move on to a new place with his family when it was time to leave?

Two sisters were caring for their mother in her last days at the hospital when someone came into the room and wrote "Christ" on the bulletin board in place of the nurse's name who was to care for her that day. When the sisters pointed out the "mistake" to the nurse assigned to her care and inquired about changing it, the nurse looked at it and replied, "No, let's leave it that way." You will never convince those two sisters that anyone but Christ tended to their mother on that last day of her life.

When Dennis was a young boy, he and his dad cleaned their church in the evenings to add needed income to their family. When they were finished, they would climb the stairs into the choir loft, where his dad would play all his favorite songs on the organ. Not church hymns but his favorite songs from the thirties and forties, the most cherished of which was "Anna." On September 11, 2001, Dennis found himself in Nassau unable to get home following two planes hitting the Twin Towers in New York. He caught a flight to Freeport, jumped on a cruise ship at midnight with hundreds of other people, and was ushered into a lounge. The very first song the band played as he prayed about getting home safely to his family was "Anna," a song he had not heard in forty years. Do you think it was a coincidence that the band played that song? Dennis knew better, and the comfort and ease he felt told him that God and his dad were with him. How well God knew what would comfort Dennis the most.

Irving was a ninety-three-year-old Jewish friend who had professed to be an atheist all his life. He was not raised in the faith of his ancestry, and every conversation, usually started by him, led to why God did not exist. Irving had lost two wives, one in her youth and one later in life, and two children, one at birth and one at twelve years old. He could not reconcile his heart or mind with a God who would take little ones so young or allow a young wife and mother to suffer. Irving became very much part of our family during the last twelve years of his life. He shared all holiday meals with us and often read a personally written prayer, which he said before meals without being asked, all the while saying he did not believe in God.

He became very close to one of our sons and his young family and was excited to know a new little boy was about to be born. In the last few weeks of Irving's life, John Christopher came into the world amid many challenges, and there was a question as to whether he would live. Irving was devastated. He called one morning to say, "From this day forward I am going to pray that God will heal John Christopher completely and make him well, and although I have never believed in Him, I think He will listen to me; we are related, you know." Two weeks passed and the baby began to thrive, and Irving was ecstatic. I was sitting with him the day before he died, and he said to me, "Trudy, you know I have not believed there really is a God all my life, but now that John Christopher is well again, I think there must be, because He heard my prayer and answered me." Irving died less than twenty-four hours later.

Does the story of Jesus's death on the cross and His acceptance of the man on His right come to mind here? God stays with us intimately until we turn our hearts and minds to Him and see Him face-to-face. He draws us in any way He knows we will come—even through the birth of a brand-new baby. I am more than certain that Irving now knows the fullness of God's redeeming love for all of His children, including himself. Following Irving's death, I found many articles and writings about the existence of God among his papers. Apparently Irving had been looking for Him all his life.

A year and a half after my sister died, I had a very sweet dream. Maureen was sitting quietly in a small room. My mother and sisters were with us. Maureen looked to be about twenty-one and very, very pretty with dark brown wavy hair. She had a sweet smile on her face, and her hands were holding a small book of pictures. I was talking to her about all the places she could move to, naming the cities where each of us lived. She smiled and, pointing to a picture in the book she was holding, said, "This is the castle I am going to live in." Jesus told us that in His house, there are many dwelling places. Maureen had found the one He had chosen for her.

When Jesus tells us He is always with us, He means exactly that. He is *always* with us. Waking or sleeping, loving Him or being far away from His love, choosing to listen to Him or ignoring Him, we can't change the fact that God is always with us. God never wants to be away from us, not even for a moment. Look for Him, recognize Him, spend time with Him, love Him. If you allow Him, He will be the best friend you will ever have.

Trudy Harris, RN, was a hospice nurse for many years, moving on to become president of the Hospice Foundation for Caring. During those 22 years she continued to play a very natural role for her as a nurse, in helping people to enter the Hospice program when she knew it would be helpful and appropriate for them to do so. At the same time Harris took on additional roles in marketing, public relations, fund-raising, and development, raising more than 45 million dollars in capital contributions for the HFC. These successes enabled the organization to establish a residential care facility for 24 patients and an in-patient facility within a local teaching hospital for 28 patients, to obtain property for a third facility for patient care, and to create an Educational Institute through which physicians, nurses, social workers, and other medical professionals are trained in the understanding of end-of-life and Hospice care. She was hired by the local Hospice when it was serving 6 to 10 patients and retired when they had more than 950 terminally ill and dying patients in their care every day. She retired feeling that the work to which God had drawn her many years before had been accomplished. She is now living in Jacksonville, Florida, with her husband and enjoys traveling, reading, being with friends and family, and loving her five grandchildren, with two new little ones on the way.

TRUE STORIES OF HOPE AND PEACE AT THE END OF LIFE'S JOURNEY

"As I read this book, I cried, I laughed, and I thought . . . of my own mortality. This collection of stories transcends generations and time. What wonderful stories Trudy has given us and what a wonderful gift to those who will read this book."

—BOB LOSURE,
former CNN *Headline News* anchor

An ideal gift of
comfort and hope

NEW YORK TIMES BESTSELLER
MORE THAN 4 MILLION COPIES SOLD

A TRUE STORY
of DEATH AND LIFE

90
MINUTES IN
HEAVEN

DON PIPER
WITH CECIL MURPHEY

CPSIA information can be obtained
at www.ICGtesting.com
Printed in the USA
LVHW08s2132070818
586313LV00001B/27/P

9 780800 734404